Advance Reviews

"*All the Pretty Shoes* is a definite page turner. It is an incredible story of survival and the ability to overcome."
—ELLEN BASS, Artist-Designer

"Even days after reading the memoir *All the Pretty Shoes*, I am still swirling in my head about this incredible life story. As a mother of a child who was 12 at one time, I certainly empathized, as well as was in awe of what the 12-year-old Marika had to endure. Her life's journey with all its drama, perils and so little love made me want to hold her as I turned every page to read this remarkable journey of survival.

The painted shoes on the cover sets the tone for the flavor of this old-world saga and the Victorian-ish filligree-like lines that divide the chapters and adorn the photos further set the mood of Marika'a life in war-torn Europe."
—LINDA F. GUIFFREDA BAKER, Professor of Art and History

"An important book on the dark side of the human condition, and how we can rise above the darkness and move into the light. Very powerful. A must read."
—DAVID P. RUSSOTTO, Director of Business Development

"Marika Roth has given us a memorable account of a time that cannot be forgotten. This gripping journey is skillfully recounted in this moving adventure of love, perseverance, and personal growth. Her intelligent and readable recollections are from a person who is tender and sophisticated."
—PROF. RONALD F. TRUGMAN

"I loved the book! Made me appreciate that life's detours and road blocks are never to be feared, but overcome, because new adventures await ahead. What an interesting life you've lived!"
—AARON COHEN, VP of American Maintenance Business

"I could not put *All the Pretty Shoes* down! It is an amazing story about personal tragedy and triumph and the strength of the human spirit. Marika Roth's powerful words capture her readers from the very first page and do not let go until the very last word!" —SHARON HOWARD, Law firm

"I didn't want to put the book down, a REAL page turner! Your heartfelt description of your life struggles gave me the chills; I could feel your pain and, at other times, your happiness."
—CAREN LABOWITCH, Director of Patient Relations

"A 'must read' for every generation to come. It is a poignant story of the indomitable spirit of a 12-year-old, swirled up in the unimaginable evil world of the Holocaust in early 1945. Through sheer determination and cunning, she survives the horrors— alone. It stands out from among the many books written about the Holocaust years, in that it follows the saga of that girl into womanhood, and portrays a life that could have been stained and ruined by those years, which instead, through an unfathomable strength of survival, circumvented inner and outer battles, searched for, and achieved, a measure of happiness."
—STEFAN POLLACK, President, The Pollack PR Marketing Group

"*All the Pretty Shoes* is the remarkable story of the most remarkable woman I have ever known. Instead of defeating her, the losses, trials, horrors, and deprivations she endured made her into a strong and courageous woman who is also quick-witted, charming, and warm; a woman who finally found the love she sought. 'Compelling' is the word that best describes *All the Pretty Shoes*; once I started reading it, I simply could not put it down."
—SANDRA MCGREGOR, USC Alumni of Film

"An amazing story of survival through sheer will and determination conquering multiple tragic traumas, both physical and psychological. The book is a testament to one woman's humanity and strength." —LYNN & STEVE LIPTON, ESQ.

"L'auteur, mélange la malchance, l'obstination, le courage dans sa recherche permanente du bonheur, souvent deçu ou trahi mais qui n'abandonnera jamais. Une 'Cosette' toujours à la recherche de son Marius!" —NORBERT BLANC, France

"One comment on your book: Wow! The trials and tribulations of your youth are incomprehensible to me, a middle class American who was totally insulated from the world in which you grew up! Your story is truly remarkable."
—JIM DURFEY, Director of American Assets

"I felt as if I were reliving Marika's journey through every stage of her life—wanting to protect the orphaned child during the war, to encourage the adolescent in her school years, and to befriend her in her adulthood. An unforgettable journey of courage, hope and love." —PATI FREUD, *Independent*

"A rollercoaster ride of tragic events with an underlying spirit of determination and self-discovery through the eyes of Marika. *All the Pretty Shoes* is a gripping memoir that is impossible to put down. Amidst all the devastating events in Marika's life, I was captivated by her tenacity and strength to never give up. Hope and inspiration are central themes throughout the novel and readers will find themselves rooting for Marika to pull herself from the ashes and keep moving forward on her journey."
—DAVID N. TUASON, Financial Consultant

"I was privileged to read *All the Pretty Shoes* and quite honestly had a difficult time putting it down. Your story is certainly compelling, especially with what you needed to do to survive. As I read your journey from childhood through adolescent to today, your determination and courageous spirit was humbling. You are truly an inspiration to everyone."
—SUSAN BURSK, Century City Chamber of Commerce

"A fascinating firsthand account of a truly remarkable life. Profoundly moving and life affirming." —HUGH GRIFFIN

"*All the Pretty Shoes* takes you on a poignant and personal journey through history. Marika Roth's account of her haunting childhood and fight for survival as an adult, leave the reader both transfixed and inspired. A must read!" —STEPHANIE BOWEN

"I loved *All the Pretty Shoes*. Found it hard to put down. It is a story of survival and having to overcome obstacles during one's life. The fact that Marika survived and made it through was a testament to her flourished character. I am recommending it to everyone." —SUZANNE MARLOW

All the Pretty Shoes

by
MARIKA ROTH

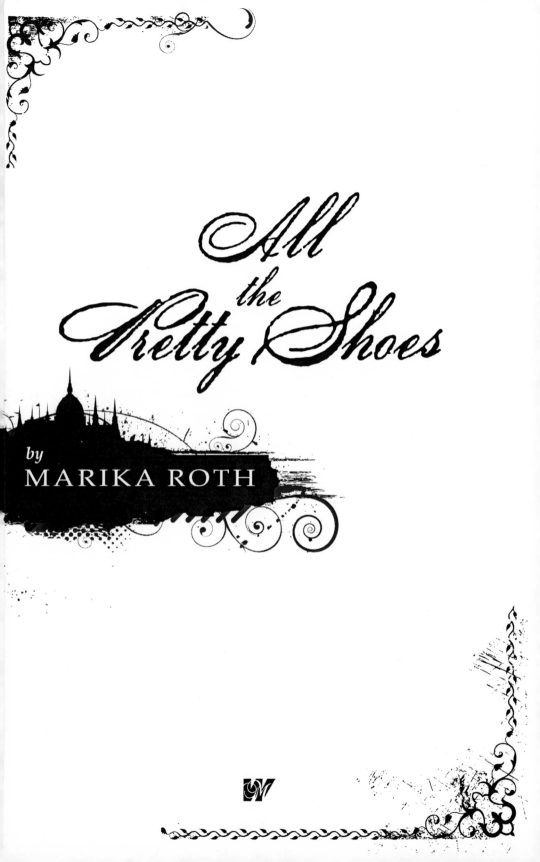

For Elizabeth and Harry,
my two formidable children,
with all my love ~
and to Suzanne, my daughter-in-law,
and Alexis, my granddaughter

M A R I K A   R O T H

All the Pretty Shoes by Marika Roth

F I R S T   E D I T I O N

ISBN: 978-1-936214-27-3
Library of Congress Control Number: 2010934356

Edited by Lisa Pliscou

Cover Painting "Budapest Hohlcaust Memorial II" by Marcus Krackowizer

M

Wyatt-MacKenzie Publishing, Inc.
15115 Highway 36, Deadwood, Oregon 97430
541-964-3314 ★ www.wyattmackenzie.com

Acknowledgements

For most of my adult years my ambition has been to write, but I never dared tackle my memoirs because that meant having to recollect the various episodes of the past I tried so hard to forget. But with the encouragement of many of my dearest friends, and perhaps also in hopes of leaving a legacy for my children, I gathered the courage that was needed.

Coming face-to-face with myself was an adventure. In the process of opening Pandora's box, I discovered a world of hidden treasures within me—forgiveness, bravery, love, and understanding—that I never knew existed.

My journey into the past has been a painful process, but it has also been enriching—if for no other reason than for the fact that my two children will have a better insight into the mother who brought them into this world. This book is, therefore, dedicated first and foremost to my son Harry Joe Klein and my daughter Elizabeth Moren, who are responsible for my reason for living.

It would be impossible to thank everyone deserving. Nevertheless, I'd like to acknowledge these extraordinary persons, my closest and dearest friends: the late Len Lipton, and my cherished friends Margaret Stokes-Rees and Louise Tougas who have been my constant inspiration for the past decade and who believed in me when I did not believe in myself. I also want to thank Ellen Bass, Sandra McGregor, Beverly Ponder, Judy Bartek, and Lorraine Jackson, who never stopped giving me their support. Above all I want to recognize Robert Morgan Fisher to whom I express my deepest gratitude for his guidance and incredible support. He has been my inspiration.

I want to thank Nancy Cleary of Wyatt-MacKenzie Publishing who believed in me, as well as my wonderful editor, Lisa Pliscou, who turned the text into perfection.

My eternal gratitude goes to Joyce Burditt, who made my project come alive, and without whom this book would have never been born.

And finally, I want to encourage all the misplaced orphans in the world to always believe in themselves and never give up their hopes and dreams.

Contents

CHAPTER 1

Massacre in Budapest

I WILL NEVER FORGET that cold winter afternoon on January 8, 1945, when I watched hundreds of Jews in the Swedish-protected housing complex rounded up by the Arrow Cross execution brigade and dragged away, regardless of their age or gender, to the banks of the Danube. I was twelve years old.

I had moved into the Swedish-protected housing shortly after my escape from the roundup of hundreds of Jews in a park near the yellow-star–tagged housing from where my father was taken. One morning, without warning the Germans had busted into our courtyard, rounded up all the men from the building, shoved them into trucks with bayonets pointed at their backs, then hauled them off to an unknown destination. As my mother was dead and I had no other family to turn to, once my father was taken from me, I was left to fend for myself. I became a lone fugitive—forever on the lookout for a place to hide without being detected or killed.

In some ways, being a child was in my favor for it made it relatively easy for me to melt into places where I did not belong. In the chaos we lived under, everyone thought I belonged to someone else. So it was that while others had to pay a large sum of money to live in the Swedish protection housing, I was able to slip in unnoticed and stay for free, my very presence making people believe that I had a right to be there.

There were hundreds of people from the upper class who had given up their life's savings to buy into the Swedish protection program. To them it was like investing in their lives, for after all, they were made to believe that they would be safe and protected under Swedish law from Nazi persecution. And because there were a limited number of these houses, they soon became terribly overcrowded. To make room for all these desperate people hanging on to their lives, all the furniture in the apartments was taken out and put into piles in the downstairs courtyard. Soon we found ourselves huddled together like penguins—men, women, and children of all ages who together shared a common goal: to try to keep warm, fight off hunger, and stay alive. Yet for all our efforts to keep ourselves from freezing, it was clear we needed some added heat, especially since young and old all slept next to each other on bare floors. Finally, a collective decision was made by the family heads to sacrifice their cherished, expensive furniture. It was chopped up and thrown into the fire, because at the end of the day all that mattered to us was to stay warm.

The fact that we were harbored under the Swedish-protected housing system gave us some degree of security. We lived under the assumption of safety, which in turn gave us courage and some modicum of hope for the future. On the evening before my story begins, I don't think any of us, as we sat by the fire trying to keep ourselves warm, suspected the horrific fate that was awaiting us.

BUDAPEST JEWISH WWII MEMORIAL
SHOES ON RIVER

It happened late afternoon when without the slightest warning—
as was the Fascists' usual modus operandi—the Nazis and the
Arrow Cross army (comprised of Hungarian Nazi sympathizers
who for the most part were more merciless than the Germans
themselves) invaded our housing complex. Judging from their
commands it didn't take long for any of us to realize that the
Germans had broken their treaty with the Swedish government.
In their eagerness to kill as many Jews as they could find, large
groups of soldiers barged into our four-story apartment building
and forced all the tenants to step out onto the communal balcony

with hands held high. Pointing their rifles in our direction, the soldiers stood at attention waiting for their leader's command. Then, at the sound of the word *"Aufeuern!"* the soldiers obediently aimed their machine guns and sprayed their bullets into the helpless victims who stood humbly awaiting their inevitable death.

As soon as I heard the first shot, I let myself fall to the ground. Still, I was able to see and to hear people's cries. Dozens of victims folded like paper dolls; their lifeless bodies fell, one by one, and piled on top of each other in a pool of blood, while I lay motionless, feigning my death. I shut my eyes and tried to block off the sound of gunshots by pretending that I was someplace else. After all that had happened to me, I was an expert at being able to shut out reality by turning to happy memories and by fantasizing.

On this particular occasion I thought of a movie my father once took me to see. It was an American movie called *Sun Valley Serenade*, in which Sonja Henie skated on ice in a lovely, shiny costume. The pine trees around her were all lit up like Christmas trees, making the scene magical. I promised myself that I would not rest until one day I could immigrate to America just like Sonja Henie.

But soon I was awakened from my daydream by a harsh kick to my rib cage. Knowing full well that my life hung in the balance, I forced myself to remain limp and motionless without showing my pain. The soldier who had kicked me with his boot was easily satisfied by my lifeless appearance and since there were so many other bodies he needed to inspect, he quickly moved on. I lay still in that same spot, without moving a muscle, long after darkness set in. In a strange way I felt safe lying there, assuming that since everyone was dead the soldiers would not return, but after a while that eerie silence became unbearable and I was eager to move on.

It was clear that I was the only survivor. Wasting no time I rose from the dead, climbed over their bodies, ran down the stairs from the second floor, then slipped into the dark street with the stealth of an accomplished burglar. Realizing that apartment buildings were unsafe, this time I was headed toward a nearby park along-side the Danube, where I remembered Mother would often take me to listen to Sunday concerts of Johann Strauss music when I was a toddler.

Being familiar with the park, I knew it had many bushes so I was confident that I could find a safe hiding place. I selected a bush at the very edge of the park closest to the Danube and brushed away my footprints in the snow; then, camouflaged by the branches, curled up like a cat and settled in for the night, trying to keep warm and nursing my sore side from the soldier's kick. I thought about what had happened earlier in the day and I congratulated myself, knowing how proud my parents would have been of me for my bravery and my cleverness. I thought about my mother and how she couldn't possibly have survived this terrible war. For the first time since I lost her, I was actually glad that she was no longer alive. It was comforting to know that she at least did not have to be exposed to humiliation and torture. She had been so fragile, so delicate.

It also felt reassuring to remember some of the tender moments Mother and I shared together during our better days, before she became ill with tuberculosis. I recalled the times the two of us walked arm-in-arm along the fashionable avenues, looking at all the pretty shoes and dresses in shop windows. Mother was opposed to buying ready-made clothes or shoes. To her it was just as inconceivable as wearing fake jewelry. People of class only wore real jewelry and tailor-made shoes and clothes. Accordingly all my clothes and shoes had to be hand-made to which I objected heartily since I resented having to stand—for what I considered to be hours—for proper fittings.

I cherished the times Mother confided in me that I was her best friend, for I admired her beauty, her slim figure, and her elegant manner—all of which made me feel proud that she was *my* mother and my friend. Compared to other children whose mothers were so ordinary, I felt like the luckiest child on the planet. At times I wondered if I could or would ever take after her when I grew up.

Then there were the times when Mother and I would stroll along the banks of the Danube, not far from where I was hiding, and listen to gypsies play their tambourines and violins, sending out their young children to solicit money from the people listening. Their costumes always fascinated me with their layers of multi-colored skirts, ornamented with lots of fake jewelry. There was never a time when Mother did not turn men's heads as we passed by. In this very park was where, in my younger years, I used to chase pigeons. Mother would say, "You can only catch them if you throw salt on their tails." I recalled her delightful laughter as she playfully teased me with the prospect.

My thoughts turned to my father. I wondered how far the Germans had taken him from me, and if he were still somewhere in Budapest. I worried about the Germans hurting him and about how we would find each other again once all this madness was over. We should have made plans but then again we were never even given a chance to say goodbye to each other. He was taken away so quickly. I decided that we would simply return to the house from where he was taken—which to me made perfect sense. Finally, comforted by this thought, I found my eyes closing from exhaustion. I must have dozed off, because the next thing I heard were harsh commands both in German and in Hungarian, followed by the familiar sound of machine guns.

It was freezing cold that foggy dawn near the Danube, but my fear of being discovered kept me perfectly still. As I peeked through the bushes, I witnessed a horrendous sight. A long row of Jews—men, women, and children—was lined up along the edge of the river. While I could not see their faces, I could see their shoes well enough to recognize that these were shoes of good quality, belonging to the members of an affluent society. Yet regardless of their stature, there they stood, humbled and humiliated in the last moments of their lives. I could hear their loud agonizing cries as they begged for their lives. But their pleading fell on deaf ears and before long the soldiers of the Hungarian Arrow Cross aimed their rifles and shot them point blank. Hundreds of limp bodies fell straight into the cold waters of the Danube.

My heart ached for those victims even as I held my breath for fear of being discovered. Suddenly I found myself thinking, *Do I even want to live in this kind of misery? How long can this war last? Isn't there anyone out there who can save us?* From my vantage point I could both see and hear some of the lifeless bodies fall into the river, tinting the blue Danube deep red with the endless flow of their Jewish blood.

I covered my eyes. I couldn't understand the reason for all the hatred that was so suddenly directed at us. What was so terrible about being Jewish? How were we different from anyone else? What could the Jews have done to deserve such cruel execution? I suddenly hated myself for who I was. For a brief moment I became my own Nazi, wishing I had been born someone else. I was living in this terrible nightmare all the while hoping that I would soon awake in the arms of my parents and all my misery

GRANDPARENTS AND THEIR FOUR CHILDREN
MOTHER IS NEXT TO HER BROTHER GEORGE

would be over. But there was no time to reflect on my feelings. I knew that if I wanted to stay alive to see my father again I had to remain focused on my survival—to find a way out of this hell and move on.

Realizing that my chances of escaping death in the city were practically nil, I decided to head for the outskirts of Budapest where I assumed Jews were less likely to be persecuted, since they were far fewer in number. Once again I waited till sunset. Then I took off on foot toward my grandfather's house in the outskirts of

Budapest, in a town called Angels Pasture. While I walked on my lengthy journey, I reflected once again on my narrow escape from death, and began to believe that perhaps my mother or some sort of unknown forces were protecting me. How else could I have managed, over and over again, to survive? I began to wonder who I was. How and why did I get here?

CHAPTER 2

From the Beginning

BUDAPEST, HUNGARY, 1912. The year my mother was born was still part of that romantic era when men courted women with flowers and gifts, and young ladies were still chaperoned to dances. Women wore pretty lace dresses and bows in their hair, and they conducted themselves with refined elegance.

This was a city that provided the finer things in life: the opera, the ballet, and the free park concerts. The number-one song was "Alexander's Ragtime Band" and the Charleston was the craze. The monarchy was still in power, and the class system was still very much entrenched.

Long considered one of the most beautiful cities in Europe, Budapest offered many elegant cafés with outside terraces, marvelous promenades lined with fine old trees and welcoming shade with sequestered areas where lovers could steal an occasional kiss. Seven bridges crossed the Danube from Pest, the city, to Buda, the mountainside. One bridge led to the long and narrow Margaret Island. With its large hotel, coffeehouses, traditional Turkish baths where one could get a fabulous massage, its warm sulphur springs, restaurants, and public swimming pools, Margaret Island was like an escape to paradise.

Not unlike Paris, Budapest was a place for lovers. Legend had it that at one of the fashionable cafés, a young engineer once approached a woman, unaware she was married, and asked her for a date, whereupon the husband, hearing of the incident, challenged the young man to a duel and shot him dead on the spot with a single bullet. Had such been the practice in my grandmother's social circle, she would have likely caused the death of numerous young men in their pursuit of her favor, since Grandmother was a huge flirt. It was well known that her weakness was men, and her love for them was not curtailed even following her marriage to my grandfather.

Mother was born in the month of December just a couple of weeks short of Christmas. The day was cold, not just because of the season, but because her arrival was unwelcome. She was the fourth child, and only her brother and sisters gathered around her crib, happy to celebrate the new addition to the family. My grandmother wanted nothing to do with this baby who had arrived in the midst of her pursuit of a divorce from my grandfather.

As the years passed and Mother grew into her teens, Grandmother never missed a chance to tell her that she was unwanted, that she had been nothing more than an accident. At times she even teased Mother by telling her she was adopted. So lacking in parental love was she, that at the age of fifteen, Mother swallowed a handful of pills, intending to end her miserable life. Instead of showing regret and compassion, her angry parents scolded her severely, and blamed each other for their daughter's suicide attempt. This incident caused a family uproar, and ultimately, my grandfather packed his bags and moved out even though their divorce had not been finalized. To this day I don't know if it ever even was.

Since there was not much money in the family, Grandfather moved with his ninety-year-old father to a suburb called Angels Pasture, a small working-class district outside of Budapest where less expensive housing was to be had. Grandmother, on the other hand, already had her new man lined up, and it wasn't long before she shacked up with him.

Following the family breakup, Grandmother's only son, George, moved from Hungary to France, where he eventually settled down and married a French woman. Grandmother's first child, Ella, died at an early age of cancer of the larynx, leaving Grandmother with two of her four children nearby, my mother and her middle daughter, Klari—her favorite.

Living with a dysfunctional family was not easy for my mother, who was sensitive and kind by nature. Being continually abused by her mother, even after her failed suicide, still caused her to question herself whether she wanted to live or die. As a means of escaping her misery, she made it her business to get out of the house, away from her mother, and socialize in cafés. It was on one of these occasions whereupon she met my father.

Father was so consumed by gambling that he was still a bachelor as he was nearing forty. He had never thought much about getting seriously involved with women since gambling was not just his profession but also his passion. Yet as soon as he saw my mother, he was so smitten by her beauty and charm that he was prepared to sacrifice all and change his life forever.

Mother was seventeen when she blissfully accepted my father's proposal of marriage. Father saw her as a young, vivacious, exciting young woman full of ambition, hardly realizing that she was at the end of her recovery period from attempted suicide. When Father arrived in her life, she saw him as her knight in shining armor. This was her prince who, with his proposal of marriage, instantly liberated her from her wretched family life.

Because of my father's reputation as a gambler, and the fact that he was twenty-three years older than my mother, both sides of the family disapproved of their relationship. Although no one seemed to have cared about them before, now suddenly everyone had a say in how this apparently loving "young" couple should manage their lives. But my parents ignored their warnings, and in December, shortly after Mother's seventeenth birthday, they took their marriage vows. It was a small civil ceremony attended only by the necessary witnesses.

Father, who was exceptionally gifted in his trade, did well most of the time. As a result, the newlyweds happily settled into a lovely apartment in an upscale Budapest neighborhood. Mother quickly became accustomed to the finer things in life, and even hired a German nanny, this being the practice in elite circles, one year after I was born. By the time I was able to form sentences I was fluently bilingual in Hungarian and German.

To the best of my knowledge, my parents enjoyed their marital bliss for only a short period. My father worshiped my mother, and she adored her comfortable lifestyle. But as with all addictions, even with the best of intentions promises are broken. Following their brief honeymoon, Father gradually began to fall back into his old profession, since he was not much good at anything else. Within a year after my arrival, it became clear that this marriage had not been made in heaven.

Unlike Father, Mother had ambitions to ascend socially. She hated what she considered the bourgeois gambling sphere in which Father moved. While his life revolved around horses, coffee-houses, and casinos, her passion was all about elegance, culture, and refinement. Fortunately for her, her looks and charm allowed her a natural entree into high society, where she was at her best mingling with influential people. Mother in her twenties was in love, not with my father but with the intellectual stimulation of the arts, theater, opera, museums, high fashion, and the overall atmosphere of the elite.

Though Father must have known this about Mother before he married her, he was much too intoxicated by her charm and beauty to pay attention to the warning signs. It had to have been apparent that his proposal of marriage was just a convenient ticket out for Mother, an escape from her miserable existence. But being the gambler that he was, he took a chance—perhaps naively believing that in time she would learn to love him and accept him for who and what he was.

A year following their nuptials, the joy that came with my birth temporarily numbed and distracted them from their brewing conflict. In spite of their failing marriage, they were both excellent parents. Father was a gentle soul, loving and caring, and as far as I was concerned his gambling for me was a benefit. Although he was seldom home to tuck me into bed at night, he never forgot to leave me part of his winnings on the night table with a note that read: *I love you.* He adored me, and was never hesitant to let me know. Oftentimes he would sing me his favorite Hungarian ballad: *"There's one little girl in the world and she is my darling turtledove. God must have loved me very much for giving her to me."*

MOTHER & ME

From my youthful perspective, both my parents loved me equally; I was the focus of their attention. As if to compensate for her unhappy childhood, Mother gave me the depth of love she never received as a child. I returned her affection in kind by being obedient. She would read me fairy tales every night at bedtime, some of which she had written herself. With her beautiful stories about princesses who lived in magnificent castles, she was able to both entertain and subtly educate me as to her expectations for me.

Each of my parents let me know how important I was to them, and that made me feel very special. Without realizing it at the time, I was the catalyst that held their marriage together—at least, until I was five. It was their consistent love and devotion for me during those years that later gave me the tools to survive, and that sustained me throughout the rest of my life.

* * *

When I was six, I became terribly sick with diphtheria. As my condition weakened to the point where I could no longer walk or get out of bed, the doctors suggested that I be taken to a higher altitude to strengthen my overall condition. Mother immediately took measures to move me to the mountains where we checked into a four-star hotel that was located right at the foot of a magnificent mountain. There I was bedridden for some time until at length I was able to walk to the window, where I spent my time enviously watching children of the other guests play in the garden.

There were many crows in the garden, and Mother would tell me stories about how crows like to steal gold and shiny objects, which is why many of them lived in palaces. Mother's wonderful stories kept me entertained for a while, until finally I became strong enough to join the other children in the garden.

On one of these occasions, while my friends and I were playing hide-and-seek, one kid suggested that we climb over the four-foot brick wall that was separating the garden from the vast mountain, just to see what lay ahead. Without further ado, everyone started to climb, their strong healthy legs carrying them far into the distance, while I in my weakness straggled behind. It was then that suddenly a young man appeared from nowhere and said, "Would you like me to help you catch up to your friends?" Without waiting for my reply, the young man took my hand and began dragging me toward the bushes in the opposite direction. As soon as I felt his strong grip, I sensed that I was in danger. I tried to free myself but it was too late. He threw me on the ground and started ripping off my pants. As weak as I was, I fought back with all my might, and while kicking and scratching I must have accidentally kicked him in the groin for all at once he let go of me, giving me an opportunity to get up and run.

How I made it back to the hotel with no more than scratches is still a miracle. All I know is that someone who saw my pitiful condition called for my mother, who appeared in a flash, rushed me upstairs to our room, called a doctor, put me in a hot bath, and notified the police. Following this incident, Mother sat me down and took it upon herself to educate me about the 'birds and the bees' and about how women and men were different, and that private parts were to remain very secret from strangers' hands.

*   *   *

From 1932 to 1935, a political power struggle was waged in Hungary between the liberal conservatives and the radicals of the far right. In 1935, the far right gained the upper hand, and this was to have a profound—and disastrous—effect upon the Hungarian Jewish community.

This was also the period when my parents finally separated and then divorced, causing my personal paradise to crumble. Mother wanted exclusive custody so she could keep me at a safe distance from Father's gambling and his casino lifestyle. I instantly became the prize in a raging contest being fought in the name of parental love. It was increasingly difficult for me to know which of my parents to believe: which one to love, when and even how to love each of them. But because children are generally resilient by nature, it wasn't long before I learned to forgive them and to love each of them just as they had loved me—unconditionally.

Our lives began to settle into a pattern, and soon I learned to enjoy my dual existence. I enjoyed watching horse races with my father as much as I enjoyed going to the opera to watch *Carmen* or *La Traviata* with my mother. Father shared his tenderness, his love, and his winnings with me, while Mother taught me integrity and introduced me to culture and high society. I was a happy child.

Then, suddenly, one day a string of dark clouds settled over our already broken family when my twenty-two-year-old mother was diagnosed with tuberculosis. At first, Father and I thought her symptoms were due to a common cold, but when her coughing failed to subside, it raised our suspicions. I will never forget the day I found my mother bent over the bathroom sink, pale-faced and weak, coughing up blood. I was horrified and my knees were shaking.

Feeling helpless and frightened, all I could do was continually pray. *Now I lay me down to sleep ... Please take care of my mother!* But as I observed the slow deterioration of my mother's beauty and youth, I suspected that God wasn't listening. Even though I was only eight at the time, it was clear to me that our lives were about to take a drastic turn for the worse. My emotions were a jumble of fear, anger, loneliness, self-pity, shame, and pride. Bearing witness to my mother's suffering instantly robbed me of my childhood—not just because she came down with tuberculosis, but also because I became *persona non grata.* Everyone who knew the facts of my mother's illness was afraid to come near me. I had become a society outcast.

A great deal had changed in those few years since I was born— the period shortly after the Great Depression and prior to World War II. For many, life was still carefree and comfortable. The Charleston was replaced by the jitterbug, and women became increasingly liberated. Nylon stockings were still a novelty. Fashion was becoming more daring, challenging the old traditions, allowing for the exposure of body parts never before seen in genteel company. Yet formality still had the upper hand. Women were still expected to wear long, elegant evening gowns for the theater, and men were still opening doors for ladies. Female performers were frowned upon, and acting was not seen as a respectable profession. Kissing on the first date was absolutely verboten. And although women had made some measure of progress toward equality, they were still not permitted such liberties as smoking or driving a car.

In the world with which I was familiar, people lived respectful, structured existences. They knew the rules and were pleased to abide by them. All that changed by the time I turned six or seven. Gradually our frivolous, flirtatious lives were darkened by the thoughts of war, especially in the wake of Germany's invasion of Poland. Folks who, in the past, had lived merry lives now visited coffeehouses, not for the usual superficial chatter with friends, but to seek out discussion and exchange serious speculation on the impending conflict with a rapidly approaching enemy. There were a lot of rumors about how and when the Germans would advance their troops to our borders. Everyone agreed that sooner or later an invasion of our country was unavoidable.

FATHER — MOTHER & ME

We knew the clock was ticking and that it was only a matter of time before we were headed for great danger. Although I was just a child, I could see the decline in the quality of our lives. I watched people pointing fingers at Jews; the very word "Jew" became pejorative. The Jews were encouraged to congregate amongst themselves, or, at the very least, stay humble. So began the establishment of segregation. Even the monarchy was not spared. This became evident when Mother's fiancée—a Russian baron who was a distant cousin of the tsar himself and a refugee from the Russian revolution—was required to conceal his identity

MY AILING MOTHER

from German sympathizers. The gaiety and laughter that once was part of our lives gradually gave way to fear, terror, suspicion, and hatred. Newspapers were reporting the imminent arrival of Hitler as if it were the coming of Christ. We could clearly see the dark clouds hover over all of us, regardless of age, race, or religion.

My parents were not a religious people. In my household, I knew of no difference between Jesus and Abraham. I had been taught one prayer, and that one went directly to one God! So, while the world outside was speculating about the coming of war, and condemning the religion of our people, our little family was focused on Mother, who was waging her own battle against death. As her condition worsened, and the prospect of spending months in a sanatorium became unavoidable, her immediate concern was not about her life, but about mine. She wanted to make certain that I was taught her sense of values before she reached her final hours. She insisted on teaching me good manners, how to be a proper lady, and how to defend myself from men and their base desires. In time, the stress that Mother endured, combined with a variety of medications, turned her into a nervous—and often-times extremely hostile—young woman. She would flare up, unprovoked, and hurt me physically. At times like that, even when I was hurting, deep down I understood that Mother was hurting more than I, and my heart and compassion went out to her.

Mother's wish for me to become an aristocrat prevailed. During her remission period, and in spite of her illness, she had become engaged to the baron. The baron loved my mother enough to want to marry her in spite of her illness, assuming, I suppose, that in time she would somehow fully recuperate. Following Mother's engagement, she made it her business to have the baron's older sister tutor me, and mold me into the lady she hoped I would become. Hence, I was introduced to the baroness whose face at first glance reminded me of a horse. But as I got to know her, I could not help but admire her exquisite, refined manner. She was kind and gentle and it wasn't long before I enjoyed her afternoon lessons about table manners, posture, polite conversations, and the value and appreciation of the finer things in life.

Mother's concerns for my well-being did not end with my education. With the steady rise of anti-Semitism, she managed despite my religion to place me into a convent, considering it to be a safe haven. She assumed that living with nuns and children my own age would protect me from religious prejudices, never suspecting that even children were capable of anti-Semitism.

CHAPTER 3

Life in the Convent

MOTHER HIRED A TAXI to take us across Margaret Bridge. We drove up and down hills for what seemed like years. Aside from Mother's occasional outburst of a sudden coughing spell, neither she nor I spoke a word during that entire journey. I suppose we were both consumed by our own private thoughts and apprehension.

The taxi stopped in front of a large iron gate. I was frightened, not just because of the convent's severe appearance, but because I also knew that in just a few moments, my mother would kiss me goodbye and leave me among a group of strangers who neither loved me nor cared about me. Worse still, there was the uncertainty of when, or if, I would ever see her again.

Once the gate opened, the taxi driver drove us up to the main entrance—to a tall building that seemed to spread far into the distance. Mother paid the fare, and we entered a marble lobby that was both cold and serene in appearance. The first thing that caught my attention was the depiction of a male figure hanging from a cross. I was shocked by this brutal image, with thorns on his head and blood dripping from the side of his face! Mother noticed my horror and told me the painting was of Jesus, who died for us. I could not understand the concept. Soon, a nun appeared in her white headgear and long black gown to welcome us and with her hands hidden inside her robe, she politely escorted the two of us to the Mother Superior's office.

Even though the nuns seemed kind and gentle, I broke into tears when Mother kissed me goodbye. At that very moment I hated her for leaving me, and for being sick. The nun took my hand. "Come," she said. "We must pick up your uniform." Her words rang in my ear loud and clear while I stared at my mother. She was about to leave. The hatred that filled my heart soon subsided and was replaced by an intense sense of love and pity for my sick mother as I watched her slim, weak figure leaving the room— leaving me with a terrible sense of loneliness.

*   *   *

Life in the convent was unlike anything I had ever known. It was regimented, strict, and of course very pious. All the children wore uniforms and were expected to walk quietly, in straight lines at all times. My mother had warned me never to reveal my true identity to anyone, but oftentimes my awkwardness, especially during prayers, or when calling the rosary or singing the hymns, made the other girls suspicious.

MOTHER BEFORE SHE WAS STRUCK WITH
TUBERCULOSIS

Gradually, I learned about—and believed in—the meaning of Christ, the reason for his crucifixion, and how the saints were there to guide us and to give us hope through our prayers. I learned how to use the rosary, how to respond to the priest's prayers; I learned the words to the songs, when to kneel, and when to stand.

I learned that by staring at the crucifix, which I did very often, I could almost feel the pain Jesus must have experienced underneath those sharp-edged thorns. To me, this was a warning about the depth of injustice of which humans were capable.

I loved the ornate atmosphere of the church. I loved the smell of incense, and the gold-framed pictures of saints that came with our prayer books. My favorite saint was Saint Thérèsa of Lisieux—the "Little Flower," who, like my mother, had also suffered from tuberculosis. I constantly pleaded to her for my mother's recovery. But as Mother's condition continued to deteriorate, I became suspicious of Saint Thérèsa's powers. It soon became clear that I was praying to deaf ears. No one was listening to my prayers.

Meanwhile, as the German army was nearing Hungary, many Hungarian Christians were shifting their allegiance to the Nazis. As such, one seldom knew who was the enemy and who was the ally; after all, we all spoke the same language. One thing remained unchanged, and that was the escalation of hatred for the Jews. I found myself having to fight my own personal battles of prejudice as the students in the convent became wise to my ethnicity. Often I would be cornered by a group of girls who would push me against the wall, tease me, and pull on my long pigtails. The result was almost always a protracted fight, where I stood alone against several attackers.

In spite of my mother's request to the administration that Father not visit me, he always managed to show up, even if just for a little while. Although he was not allowed in, he knew to stand by the garden gate where we took our scheduled afternoon walks. I would sneak over to him and he would speak words of love and reassurance; I would tell him how much I loved him too. On one of these occasions, I told Father about my unhappiness there and about the other children's abuse. Since Father had been against my living in a convent from the start, he immediately removed me from the premises by helping me climb over the fence. We left without bothering to consult Mother Superior, without even collecting my things, or notifying my mother. In so doing, Father became my ultimate hero.

* * *

My stay with Father was truly a heartening period. Up to that point, and primarily due to Mother's intervention, he and I had never spent much time together. Now that she was locked up in a sanatorium, we had the freedom to enjoy each other. Since Father didn't have a regular job, we could spend every hour of the day doing anything I wanted. He imposed no discipline and no restrictions.

Father took me to races, coffeehouses, movies; he taught me to play poker. He allowed me to stay up late and to eat as much pastry as I wanted. And he introduced me to our true heritage by taking me to the synagogue. I marveled at the disparity in religions and wondered why this was necessary when there was only one God.

I learned that unlike the church, the synagogue was lacking in ornamentation. Instead of idolizing a male figure on a cross, the

Jews idolized the Torah. Instead of meditating on the rosary, they meditated on fringes on the edge of their shawl. Women and men had to be separated, and all the prayers were in Hebrew—a language I could not understand. This lack of understanding sharply limited my ability to cultivate any feelings for Judaism. Nothing that was said in the synagogue ever touched my heart the way Jesus did from the cross.

What I loved most about my father was his warmth. I loved being able to kiss and hug him whenever I liked, and to be able to laugh and cry without shame. I loved the smell of tobacco on his clothes, and the silly brown hat with the crooked brim that he liked to wear at a jaunty angle—somehow it always became a popular target for bird droppings as he walked underneath the dozens of walnut trees that were on display on Andrassi Boulevard. I was once again a happy child.

Finally the day came when Father decided to introduce me to his side of the family. Born in a small town miles from Budapest, near the Romanian border, Father came from a family of four—two girls and two boys. One of his sisters, my Aunt Bella, and his brother, Uncle Miklos, lived in Budapest, not far from our neighborhood. My introduction to the family was a mixed success. While they were all nice and polite, it was obvious they were not comfortable in my presence—in part because of my mother's illness, and also because of their ongoing prejudice against my parents' marriage. They never really took to my mother; she was not their sort of people and vice versa. There was a class difference they could not get past. Still, there was a time when both sides of the family must have tried to get along, since I recall some photos of Aunt Bella and my mother walking side-by-side in front of the opera house. Then, as Mother's condition worsened, so did their relationship.

MOTHER & AUNT BELLA

Now, with my newly found relatives, I finally had a sense of what it was like to be part of a clan. In a short time, Uncle Miklos' daughter, Vera, who was my age, became my very good friend. Each time Father and I visited, Vera and I spent our time together playing games. Our favorite pastime was to pretend we were actors. We set up a playhouse underneath the building's staircase and improvised our own scenarios.

Mother, of course, was enraged when she found out Father had removed me from the convent, and wasted no time reclaiming her custody rights as soon as she returned home. Although she had no place for me to go, she was unwilling to compromise in her beliefs as to what was best for me. Never did she miss an opportunity to disparage Father's "low-life" gambling habit. In desperation to find me a home, Mother turned to her sister and mother for their assistance, but they both categorically refused to have me, fearing exposure to tuberculosis. She even wrote to her brother George in France who, unsurprisingly, had no intention of accepting any responsibility for me.

I was dreading my forthcoming separation from Father, who provided me with the warm affection—the kisses and the hugs—for which I was thirsting, and which Mother's illness forbade her to give me. At certain times, she was even quarantined, prohibiting any sort of physical contact. Still, there was hope that the possible removal of her damaged lung would eventually set her back on her feet. But, alas, it wasn't long before Mother was told that her second lung had become infected as well, which meant that surgery was no longer possible. Once again, she was to be admitted to the sanatorium, this time with some urgency.

Left with no alternative, Mother found an institution someplace in the outskirts of Budapest that took in children without discriminating against religion or gender. It was operated by a young couple, Mr. and Mrs. Kovacs, who, as it turned out, ran the place strictly for financial gain—which was clearly indicated by their cruel conduct toward the children.

* * *

Unlike the convent, there was very little discipline in this institution. Children did not have to wear uniforms, and they were not constantly supervised. We acted accordingly—like desperate inmates. Our survival was dependent on being the smartest, the quickest, and the strongest, and being able to withstand the severest of punishments, such as deprivation of food, or kneeling on dried corn kernels and facing the wall in a corner for long periods. Those of us who endured without tears were highly valued and respected by other children.

From the moment I set foot in the door, I could read Mrs. Kovacs' fake smile, the one she no doubt wore just to appease parents and relatives. Knowing full well that creating a fuss or pleading not to be left behind would have been futile I remained silent, but after Mother left, as I stood by the window to wave goodbye, I told myself I would leave as soon as possible.

It wasn't long before my first impression of the place was confirmed. I knew of no child who was happy there. The food was inedible, the rooms were crowded, the cots were uncomfortable, and the boys made it their hobby to torment the girls at all times. Mr. and Mrs. Kovacs' punishments involved beating us with straps or exposing us to humiliation by calling us "stupid" in front of the other children. Altogether the place reeked of fear and a hostile atmosphere. Even though I managed to make some friends, and even developed a mad crush on one of the boys who was one year older, I couldn't wait to get out of there, and went to bed every night secretly planning my escape.

After a few weeks—which felt like years—I received a letter from my mother telling me that she was out of the sanatorium and back in her apartment while in remission. This was the cue I was waiting for, and was truly, in my opinion, a godsend. Not wanting to waste a single moment, the very next day I took action.

In the dim light of early dawn I quietly slipped out of bed, got dressed, tiptoed to the first-floor window, and jumped out onto the gravel path. The Kovacs must have heard the noise from upstairs, because the moment my feet hit the ground I saw the lights turn on in their room. Seconds later, a flashlight beamed in my direction and I heard footsteps following me not too far behind.

Mr. Kovacs yelled out: "Stop where you are!"

But I refused to yield. Instead, I ran across the courtyard toward the gate with Mr. Kovacs hot on my trail. As determined as an Olympic athlete, I managed to outrun him. Quickly I scrabbled up and over the tall fence, and finally ran to my freedom across an empty field that eventually led into the village. Once there, I hopped onto the coupling of the trolley car, and headed for Budapest.

The horrified look on my mother's face when she found me standing at the door will remain in my memory forever. She very nearly collapsed. Aside from the fact that she was feeling weak, she was also considered very contagious during this period, and for that reason alone, I wasn't suppose to be anywhere near her. Although she did let me into the apartment, she gave me a strict warning between heavy tears and coughing spells to keep at a safe distance. Naturally, I was scolded severely for my escape. But once I had my say and was able to explain, Mother became compassionate and forgiving. Still, she could think of no other place to put me, and that remained her major concern.

For the following days, and until Mother was able to figure out another solution, we lived under the same roof, all the while keeping our distance as much as possible. I tried my best to act grown-up and made myself useful as a nurse, but her constant coughing and choking was beginning to wear on me. Each of her attacks felt like a stab in my heart and the bloody cloth she held to her face was a constant confirmation of her suffering. I was feeling her pain, fearing the inevitable, and waging a constant battle with my range of emotions: anger, hate, fear, and love. Yet, in spite of it all, Mother and I bonded more than ever.

While Mother lay in bed, pale and weak, she talked candidly to me, not as her nine-year-old child, but as if I were her best friend. She confessed her love for the baron, who had almost lost his life during the assassination of the tsar. She told me about her unfortunate childhood with her unloving mother, about her relationship with my Father—whom she claimed to have loved but never trusted—and about her faith in God. I learned to love and understand her, not just as my mother, but also as a whole person—as a human being.

This was also a time when I had the pleasure of meeting the distinguished baron. He was tall, slim, beautifully dressed, and elegantly polite. He very much resembled the British film star Stewart Granger. What's more, he treated me like a princess, as I had never been treated before. He bowed and kissed my hand upon meeting me, and addressed me on equal terms, not as a child. He respected my views and took them into consideration. Although in my heart I knew that he could never replace my father, there was something about him, a special quality that set him apart from everyone else I had ever met, and I soon understood why my mother fell in love with him. This made it much easier for me to love him as well.

Since the baron had many influential acquaintances, he succeeded in finding a married couple who lived in the center of district VIII in Budapest, not far from the elementary school I was attending at my mother's insistence. This couple, who were in the dental profession, agreed to rent me a bed for a reasonable sum.

However, since they were running an office during the day, they could not provide me with regular meals. I was therefore required to visit a variety of families, parents of my classmates, who took me in for a meal after school hours—not because they cared about me, but as part of their charitable effort. They enjoyed introducing me as "the poor child who has no home and we're helping her out." Naturally these kinds of introductions made me feel terrible, reinforcing the fact that I was not a regular child, but a stranger, an outsider, a charity case. I was an oddity, a remnant of society that no one wanted. I felt deeply humiliated.

GRANDFATHER WEARING THE COMPULSORY
YELLOW JEWISH STAR

It didn't take long to see that this arrangement was not conducive to my well-being. Mother, in desperation, turned to her father at long last.

Realizing the seriousness of the situation his daughter was in, and the gravity of her condition, Grandfather reluctantly consented to accept custody of me—but only if it was for a short period. As he was quick to point out, he had enough with taking care of his own father, and besides, he was not set up to raise children.

CHAPTER 4

Grandfather's House

I HAD NO RECOLLECTION of ever having met my seventy-two-year-old grandfather prior to the day Mother dropped me off at his place. She told me very little about him, so I naturally was apprehensive. All I knew was that my grandfather was poor—he earned a scanty living selling and trading bits and pieces of leather for such items as shoes and bags—and that he lived alone with his aged father. When Grandfather opened his front door and we stepped inside, all I could see was total darkness. Then, gradually, as my eyes adjusted, I saw that we were in a small dark room and that Grandfather was a tall, thin man with a black moustache and a stern face. Despite his ragged, ill-fitting black suit jacket, he carried himself with a certain dignity and pride.

Mother and I sat at the table that was placed in the center of the room. When Grandfather offered her a cup of tea she hastily replied that she could not stay long. There were a few words exchanged, mostly about me and to me, how I should be good, grateful, and obedient. Soon Mother was on her way. There were no hugs, no tears, no speeches. She simply stepped outside the door just as if she were to return momentarily. I remained seated at the table, afraid to look around. Grandfather began talking about the household chores I would be expected to do.

*   *   *

Grandfather lived in a single tiny room that he shared with his ninety-five-year-old father and, now, with me. Every inch of the sparsely furnished room was strategically used to its best advantage. The beds were placed alongside the three walls, with the cooking stove occupying the remaining space. The stove was heated by coal, and our light came from a kerosene lamp that gave out a putrid odor. The combined odors from the coal and kerosene lamp left me with a perpetual reminder of our despicable poverty. The square table, covered by an old tablecloth, sat in the center of the small room with a couple of chairs on either side. There was one small closet by the door, and a small sunken bay window overlooking the yard was the only source of natural light. Toilet facilities were public and located a couple of doors down the hall.

In a curious contrast to this squalid atmosphere, a beautiful painting hung on the wall directly above Great-grandfather's bed. The picture displayed a plush Victorian-era garden with spring flowers all around, where fashionable ladies dressed in long satin gowns and holding lace parasols sat beneath oak trees chatting, while their carefree children happily played tag on an expanse of lush green grass. A group of elegant men, dressed in striped pants and top hats and wearing monocles, stood nearby. They leaned on their walking sticks and seemed to be casually chatting amongst themselves.

Very soon that painting became my salvation. It virtually hypnotized me. It offered me a daily escape from my miserable existence, especially in the evenings when the flickering flames from the kerosene lamp transformed those images from still life into real people. Then I would allow myself the luxury of merging into that aristocratic family. This was, after all, the sort of life my mother had envisioned for me.

Grandfather was not much for small talk. From the day I moved in, aside from reminding me about the chores I was expected to do, he had very little to say. My duties consisted of cleaning house and helping with the cooking; I also read the newspaper out loud to him as he considered this a form of education for me as well as entertainment for himself. But, since I was only nine, and my education up to that point was rather limited, Grandfather would equate my poor reading abilities with stupidity. On this matter he freely voiced his opinion, comparing me critically with Aunt Klari's daughter Agi, his favorite grandchild. To make matters worse, with the war at our doorstep, and with me living a distance from the city, my formal education was put on hold indefinitely. Then there were the times when Grandfather took pleasure in testing my strength and resistance by telling sickening stories while I ate. One of his favorite stories was about a young girl, who after she ate her noodles topped with poppy seed and sugar (a favorite Hungarian dish, and one that I use to love) went walking across the street and was hit by a car. The accident caused her stomach to open and all the noodles would come out. Then someone came by and ate them. Grandfather told that story to me many times just to see if I could keep from throwing up. He despised any sign of weakness.

As for Great-grandfather, he was a worshiper of God and believed in the magic of prayers. He was a man who lived by tradition and followed a daily routine from which he never wavered. He would get up each morning at five, use his urinal, wash his hands and face in the basin, put on the same shirt and pants he wore every day of his life, then shuffle over to the window, adjust his yarmulke and his spectacles, wrap himself in the tallis, open his prayer book at the specifically marked pages, then rock back and forth repeating the same phrases in Hebrew over and over. Now and then, he would turn the pages as if he were actually reading which he could not have done due to his poor eyesight.

GREAT GRANDFATHER AT AGE 92

Following this ceremonial ritual, he'd shuffle over to his chair next to the stove, light up his long pipe, and wait for my grandfather to serve him his breakfast.

Although Grandfather was not particularly interested in religious rituals, to please my great- grandfather, he pretended to hold a kosher household. This meant never mixing dairy and meat products and having these items blessed by a rabbi before consumption. However, there were exceptions to the rule and I recall one occasion when for some reason Grandfather splurged and purchased a live chicken. He brought the poor animal home, placed it on the middle of the table as it were some great victory prize, and said to Great-grandfather, "You do the honor." Great-grandfather got out of his chair, picked up his cane, and shuffled to the window where he kept his prayer book. Clearly following some traditional ritual, Grandfather picked up the flopping, crying chicken, and handed it over to Great-grandfather, who took the chicken, lifted it into the air, then circled it around my head three times as he recited a prayer. While the frightened chicken was trying its best to break loose, in the struggle I received its droppings on top of my head. This was one of the rare occasions that I saw my grandfather smile at me as he said, "You are now truly blessed."

Once the ceremony was over, Great-grandfather shuffled back to his seat and remained silent. Grandfather took the chicken outside to cut off its head, and I sat quietly in my corner reflecting about what just happened. I could not understand the relation between the chicken and me. How could circling a resisting chicken over my head be a blessing to me? What powers could a chicken possibly have before its dying moments? It all seemed so ridiculous and much too complicated for my nine-year-old brain to comprehend. All I could think of was that soon that chicken would end up on my plate, and I knew in advance that Grandfather would not brook any refusal to partake.

My great-grandfather was a gentle, good-natured soul. Yet hardly a day went by when my grandfather didn't find something to scold him about. At those times, the old man would just sit quietly nodding in silence. It wasn't long before Great-grandfather had become my best friend. He accepted me and loved me unconditionally. He never asked questions, he never complained, and he never voiced an opinion. He simply accepted me for who I was, just a nine-year-old child who desperately needed his love.

Because my life with Grandfather was so constrictive, I welcomed any attention I could get. A neighbor, a peasant woman who lived with her daughter a few doors down the hall from us, sometimes invited me to taste her freshly baked bread. Unlike the other tenants, this woman had a separate entrance that led to a private little garden where she grew flowers and vegetables. She also kept chickens, a rooster (who woke and angered the neighbors at dawn every day), and a piglet. I loved feeding her animals, and considered them my friends.

Oftentimes, Great-grandfather and I would go out for walks following his morning prayer, and he would let me hold his wrinkled, bony hand. He had a sharp wit, and we would laugh at silly things, especially when he made unexpected remarks about pretty women.

Once back in the house, he would return to his chair, light up his long wooden pipe, and fall silent again. It was as though he disconnected himself from the gloom that surrounded us inside. Yet whenever he noticed my loneliness, he would, without fail, call me over, invite me to sit on his brittle knees, and bounce me up and down as he sang in his scratchy old voice the only song he knew: *"One potato bag, two potato bag…"* I would stare at his wrinkled face and hands, wondering how anyone could ever become that old.

Although his advanced state of decrepitude repulsed me at first, in time I learned to see past it, and loved him for who he was, just as he loved me. Then, suddenly, one morning Great-grandfather's religious ritual came to a halt. Instead of getting out of bed in his usual manner, he lay under his cover, motionless. Grandfather called out his name, but he never responded. In frustration, Grandfather shook the old man, thinking he had a hearing problem, but the old man's body was stiff and unresponsive.

This was my first encounter with death. As I stood observing Great-grandfather's peaceful expression, I wondered if he knew that he had taken with him a piece of my heart. Then I glanced at the painting above his bed, whereupon, to ease my pain, I convinced myself that he had not died at all, but simply faded into that garden paradise above his head.

*   *   *

Following the old man's passing, my mother, who was in remission again, came to visit us. When my grandfather had left the house, the two of us sat down at the table facing each other in that stark, dim room. Mother looked at me straight in the eyes and said, "Listen, you need to hear me out." Then she told me that her condition was getting worse, her attacks were more frequent, and since now both her lungs were affected she was beyond help. Then she stretched out her arms across the table and showed me her hands and said: "See my nails? They are turning purple. That's a sure indication that I am close to my death." Her words felt like a sharp knife that just stabbed through my heart. I didn't know if I should hate her for hurting me, and for dying on me, or if I should feel sorry for the agony she was going through and offer my love. I was scared and confused. Knowing that her days were numbered, Mother proceeded to paint a dismal picture of our future. She said she couldn't possibly foresee leaving me alone in this cruel world, and since none of our family members were willing to adopt me, she had devised a perfect plan. She opened her handbag and pulled out a small revolver with a mother-of-pearl handle on it. She showed it to me with pride, as if it were some sort of priceless jewel. "This," she said, "is for both of us!" I tried to hide my fear but without success. Mother quickly reassured me that before she would use the gun on me, she would have me undergo a TB test. If the test came out positive, then the gun would be for both of us: "That way we could go to heaven together." If the test results were negative, she would let me live, and place me into an orphanage. But for as long as I was to live, she urged me, she wanted me to always believe in myself. Finally, she made me solemnly promise to keep her plan an absolute secret from everyone, especially my grandfather.

On our way to Budapest for my TB test, we stopped off to visit Aunt Klari and her three children. Aunt Klari had two boys a bit younger than me, and their sister Agi, who was a year or so older and much more sophisticated than I was. Agi was beautiful child and she knew it. While I was still just an innocent nine-year-old, Agi at eleven was already kissing boys.

By this time, the German army was rapidly advancing upon our borders. Grandfather was concerned that I would become too much of a burden on him in the event of war. With my TB test results negative and my life spared, he felt justified in asking my mother to move me elsewhere at her earliest convenience. Thanks to the baron and his sister's influence, I was accepted at a Jewish orphanage for girls, even though both my parents were still alive.

CHAPTER 5

The Orphanage

PANIC AND HATRED among Hungarians quickly became rampant. By now the Christian majority bought into Hitler's propaganda and chose to surrender their own country by shifting their allegiance to the Nazis. Instead of defending their own country, Hungarian citizens elected to follow the commands of a madman and began viciously attacking Jews and their sympathizers even prior to the Germans' arrival.

Life at the Jewish orphanage was, thankfully, devoid of anti-Semitism. Girls were assigned to different groups, depending on their ages. Being ten, I was assigned to Miss Maria's section. She was a slim, middle-aged spinster with grayish hair that was tied into a bun at the back of her head, giving her a severe appearance. Miss Maria was herself an orphan and in fact had grown up in the institution, which is how she got her job. She always wore the same black straight-cut dress, and never softened the stern facial expression that successfully concealed her otherwise kind heart.

MY ORPHANAGE UNIFORM

Miss Maria's duties were to keep the girls well disciplined, ensuring that they were punctual, obedient, unobtrusive, neat, and tidy, and that they obtained excellent marks in school. She was particularly fussy about how to make a perfect bed, clean floors, and comb our hair, but the one thing she was most strict about was our shoes. They had to be well polished and "shine like a mirror," she would say, for in her opinion a pretty pair of clean shiny shoes told of the self-respect and dignity of a person. She was also strict about our uniforms. One button missing instantly qualified for punishment. Miss Maria enjoyed her work. She did her job with pride, and always insisted on prompt and polite answers to her questions, straight posture, neat appearance, and proper table manners. No one dared to contradict her, and she was treated with the greatest respect.

Our daily routine was solidly fixed just like our daily menus, which in essence gave us a feeling of security. We always knew what to expect. There were no surprises. Seating arrangements in the dining room were based upon our ages. Older girls were seated at separate tables. Our meals were so regimented that we knew the menu in advance from Monday to Sunday. If you did not care for the gulash on Monday but loved the poppy-seed noodles that were to be served on Thursday, you could give half of your gulash away to someone and she would promise to give you half of her noodles in a few days. This became a game and an opportunity to create a sense of camaraderie between friends.

Miss Maria rang the wake-up bell each morning at six on the dot, at which time we were expected to jump out of bed, throw our covers over the bedrail, and stand at attention while she walked around the room conducting her meticulous inspection. First, she examined our sheets, making certain that no one had wet her linens. Once we all met with her approval, she gave us her special hand gesture, then watched us as we made our beds. This was followed by our march into the bathroom, where the curtainless showers were lined up in a row. We all had to strip naked, a ritual that troubled me greatly, since I was extremely shy about my growing breasts. Thanks to my mother, who refused to have my hair cut since my birth, my hair was long enough to camouflage my nakedness. Once we were showered and dressed, we had one final inspection in the corridor: nails, hands, shoes, buttons, and uniforms. Finally, we got to follow Miss Maria in a single line into the dining room.

Miss Maria's bedroom was adjacent to our dormitory, with a window that allowed her to see and hear us at all times. Those she judged deserving were invited to her room on certain evenings to enjoy some special recreation time. During those sessions, we would sit around the floor in circles; Miss Maria taught us how to knit, mend socks, and crochet, as classical music was being played in the background on her record player. Many of the girls feared, and even hated, Miss Maria, but I felt privileged and proud to receive these invitations. In time, I became one of her favorite students, and was given the special honor and responsibility of making up her bed. Even some of my best friends were envious of my promotion.

I was so starved for love that I had developed a strong need for acceptance. I knew this about myself. I would go to almost any length to gain approval from my superiors as well as my room-mates. I was very good at listening and keeping secrets. I feared any type of confrontation, and could not abide being hated. To my sorrow I alienated some of the other girls due to my desperate need for attention; I would annoy them by constantly offering to make their beds or comb their hair. Somewhere along the way, however, I discovered that laughter endeared me to most people, so I learned to make fun of myself and often turned into a clown at my own expense. I so badly wanted to be accepted.

Insubordination at the orphanage was punishable by being deprived of visitors, or by being assigned to extra household duties such as kitchen work or waxing the hardwood floor in our very large dormitory. Waxing the floor by foot was one punish-ment I never minded, since I made it into a game and simply pretended that I was ice-skating. In fact, I often offered my serv-ices as a floor waxer in exchange for my roommates' friendship.

Since there were over two hundred girls living and being educated under one roof, strict rules had to be enforced to keep things in order. We all wore a navy sailor-type uniform with dark navy or black woolen stockings. Colored ribbons were allowed in our hair, and mine were usually red—my favorite color. Older girls lived in a different section from us and were all assigned to mentor younger girls. Our responsibilities as mentors included tutoring the girls in their homework, combing their hair, and making sure they were always neat and tidy. Since I was going on eleven, I was assigned to a seven-year-old girl named Teresa of whom I grew very fond. She became my little sister.

The orphanage had its own synagogue where services were held every Friday before sundown. Having earned the right to sing in the choir, I was soon given the honor of being the number-one soloist, which placed me front and center ahead of everyone else. While I did not know Hebrew, I quickly memorized the songs and the words—which I sang without knowing their meaning. All this time, I secretly carried Saint Thérèsa's picture around in my pocket; I had regained a sense of belief in her abilities and was confident that she would always be with me and guide me wherever I went. I was certain Miss Maria would not have been very pleased had she found me out.

On the day that Mother admitted me to the orphanage, she left the same instructions with the principal that she had left with the Mother Superior at the convent—absolutely no visits allowed from my father. So, even though visiting hours were permitted once a month, I never had anyone come to see me then.

But visitors' day or no visitors' day, nothing would stop my father from attending Friday services, which were open to the public. Although the choir was located in the upstairs balcony, and worshipers were seated downstairs, my father came without fail every Sabbath, just so we could see each other, even if only from a distance. Being placed front and center allowed me a clear view of my father's silly brown hat, his blue eyes, and his warm smile, which to me was the next best thing to being in his arms. We would use sign language to communicate, whereby he would let me know that he had left me his usual care package in the main lobby, behind the large marble statute of a benefactor. His package usually contained cookies, candies, and chocolates along with a note, and I would eagerly share my goodies with the girls in my dormitory in exchange for their love and friendship. Because all my friends were orphans, the fact that I had a father who came to visit me every Friday elevated me into something of a celebrity.

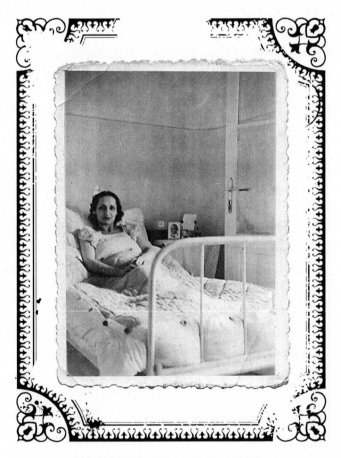

MOTHER'S LAST DAYS ON EARTH
(SEE BARON'S AND MY PICTURE ON THE NIGHT TABLE)

It was the beginning of spring, less than six months after my arrival at the orphanage, when, uncharacteristically, Miss Maria showed up in my classroom right in the middle of the lecture. As soon as she called out my name, my heart sank. The entire class-room became deadly silent. All eyes were focused on me as I sat frozen and silent in my seat. Was this to be the news I had feared for so long? I simply pretended not to hear Miss Maria's call. But in spite of my resistance I soon found myself following Miss Maria down the long corridor to the principal's office, a journey that made me feel like a criminal being led to the gallows. By the time we arrived, my head was spinning and my throat was so tight I could hardly swallow. Miss Maria opened the principal's door, allowing me to enter first which in itself was unusual, and, with my knees shaking, I walked inside only to find my stone-faced grandmother sitting there waiting for me.

The principal rose from her chair, and came to greet me with extreme politeness. She put her hand on my shoulder, gently expressing her condolences. All this time, Grandmother and I made no eye contact. She sat rigidly in her black dress, observing the principal, and then she ceremoniously exchanged the red ribbon in my hair to black, not unlike a ritual of demotion that labeled me a certified orphan. Finally, Grandmother headed for the door, expecting me to follow as she marched off like a general and announced that a taxi was waiting. Since my feet felt frozen to the ground, Miss Maria nudged me and I finally tagged behind this heartless individual who was my grandmother. As I trudged behind her I stared blankly at the outline of her wide protruding derrière underneath that black dress. It made me hate her all the more.

Mother died of tuberculosis at age twenty-eight, just two months short of the German occupation. Her funeral was very intimate.

The only people who came were the baron, his sister the baroness, Aunt Klari, Grandfather, and my father—who naturally stood at a far distance. There were some chrysanthemums placed by the side of the coffin. My recollection of that day remains very vague except for their aroma, which to me represented the smell of death.

I remember feeling a deep sense of emptiness as I stood over Mother's open grave. It was so dark, so cold. Although I shed no tears, I was overcome with a strong desire to plunge in after her, so I could hold onto her forever.

GRANDMOTHER

While prayers were being recited, I looked back on our life together, and remembered how I enjoyed my first feeling of independence at age six, when Mother allowed me to cross the street by myself under her watchful supervision. It made me feel so grown up, so independent. But now that she was gone forever, and I stood looking into that dark deep hole as her casket was lowered, my feelings were reversed. I no longer had the desire to be independent. Already I had the sense that being alone was a terrifying experience. It was no longer about crossing the road alone, but crossing my life alone without my mother. At that moment I wished that she would have used her gun, so we could have gone to heaven together.

I stood silently hating all those who came to her funeral—blaming everyone there for Mother's death. I felt that she didn't have to die. If only, if only…I hated the doctors who failed to save her life. I hated the men who were lowering her casket into that empty space surrounded by rocks and sand. I could not—did not—want to comprehend that I would never see my mother again.

As we were leaving the gravesite, I looked for my father. As soon as I spotted him, I headed in his direction, but my grandmother intercepted me. "By the way," she said coldly, "don't expect to keep anything of your mother's. I am going to have all her belongings incinerated." Her words cut through my heart like a sharp knife. If I hadn't hated her before, I most certainly did then.

But the current political events left me little time to hate anyone near me for long, since in a broader picture, the world around me was crumbling, disintegrating as if in an earthquake. People were talking about how the Hungarian police had rounded up the Jews, acting under the command of SS Colonel Adolf Eichmann, Hitler's chief and deportation expert. Thousands of Hungarian Jews were already being shoved into wagon trains that previously transported cattle. Indeed, they were treated like animals, were shoved into those wagons, and shipped to the dreaded concentration camps in places like Auschwitz-Berkenau and others in Poland, Romania, Czechoslovakia, and Ukraine. A short time later thousands of Jews from outside of Budapest were also being gathered, then shipped off in the same manner. For a time, the only Jews remaining in Hungary were the ones who lived in Budapest, although everyone knew that it was only a matter of time before our turn would come.

BUDAPEST UNDER NAZI RULE

HISTORIANS HAVE NOT PAID MUCH ATTENTION TO THE SIEGE OF BUDAPEST, WHICH WAS ON OF THE MOST BRUTAL OF WORLD WAR II. WITH GERMAN OFFICIALS EFFECTIVELY RUNNING THIS CAPITAL CITY. HUNGARIANS FACE NOT ONLY THE UNCERTAINTIES OF NAZI RULE, BUT THE CONSTANT THREAT OF THEIR OWN REPRESSIVE ARROW CROSS PARTY, A RADICAL RIGHT-WING REGIME RESPONSIBLE FOR SOME OF THE WORST ATROCITIES AFTER THE SIEGE HAD ENDED.

The first thing the Germans did when entering Budapest was to establish themselves in appropriate accommodations. The orphanage, being a large building, became one of their first targets. With its four floors, dozens of rooms, and all the amenities, it was a perfect venue for the Nazi headquarters. Without warning, we were ordered to vacate the building within a couple of hours. Orphans and teachers alike scattered in every direction, fearing for their lives.

For me, this was a wonderful opportunity to be with my father. I ran to find him at my uncle's place, taking my young protégé Teresa along with me. While Father and I were both delighted to be reunited, the danger that surrounded us kept us from fully rejoicing. Father put Teresa on the train so she could join her remaining relatives, while the two of us took refuge at my Uncle Miklos' apartment.

Cousin Vera and I were pleased to see each other again. Naively forgetting the war and the troubles around us, we set up our usual mini-theater underneath the staircase, where we acted out our original play. Sometimes we even charged admission, a penny or two. However, our fun was soon cut short with the news that all Jews were to move out of their homes and into designated areas. My father was sure that his many friends and acquaintances— Jews and non-Jews—would surely help protect us, and give us shelter. However, fearing the Nazis' retaliation for accommodating Jews, no one would volunteer their assistance, except for a middle-aged, hunchbacked spinster, Mrs. Kalamar, who had long had designs on my father. The prosperous owner of a city taxicab, the woman had nothing but money to recommend her.

CHAPTER 6

Star Houses

MRS. KALAMAR WAS A Christian woman, a card player and a gambler, and as short as she was ugly. She had squinting blue eyes and poorly dyed reddish-blond hair that looked like burnt straw. She wore bright red lipstick and doused her person in cheap perfume. It was clear to me from the moment I laid eyes on her that she wanted sole possession of my father, but to catch him, she had to offer both of us refuge at her place. It was no secret that she was insanely jealous of me right from the start.

She had a nice size apartment, conveniently located in the center of the city. Her place was filled with expensive mahogany furniture, although it was difficult to see for she had it all covered with sheets to protect it. On her walls she had a collection of poor-quality oil paintings that did nothing to lighten the gloomy atmosphere. The appalling odor—a combination of mothballs and her fetid perfume—made me want to gag. I kept pleadingly looking at my father, hoping he would pick up on my dismay, but he deliberately ignored me. Father must have known of the woman's ulterior motives when she offered her hospitality, and I suspect he sold himself to this grotesque she-devil for my sake.

Upon our arrival, the tiny Mrs. Kalamar literally slid off her chair—since her feet didn't quite reach the floor—and greeted us with what I could tell was a phony smile. My father said, "This is Marika, my daughter I told you about," and I immediately could tell that Mrs. Kalamar disliked me. My sixth sense told me that Father and I were trapped—not unlike Hansel and Gretel—in the witch's gingerbread house. To me it was inconceivable that my father could possibly love a woman as horrid as Mrs. Kalamar! The very thought made me feel deceived and momentarily lose respect for the man I so loved and worshiped. I became very confused.

Recognizing my distaste and apprehension, Father later tried to ease my fears by taking me into his arms, assuring me that staying in Mrs. Kalamar's place was only a temporary arrangement. And he was right, because by June 1944, a couple of weeks into our stay, all the Jews from the city were ordered into designated buildings marked with the yellow Stars of David. Since Mrs. Kalamar was not prepared to sacrifice herself for us, particularly since my father did not meet her expectations, it wasn't long before we were chased out of the witch's house and forced into a "yellow star" building.

These yellow-star–tagged houses were designated as the "Jewish District" and were temporary holding places for residents of the city only; Jews from the suburbs continued to be rounded up and transported to one of several concentration camps in Germany that were rapidly filling up. But at one point, the Hungarian authorities suspended deportations, thus allowing the remaining Jews of Budapest to be merely ghettoized.

Families who had originally lived in tagged apartment buildings were forced to surrender their homes in order to make room for additional families to move in on them. Consequently, quarters became increasingly cramped, and often furniture had to be removed to create floor space for people to sleep. Houses were quarantined and locked up. No one dared to walk on the streets, and every footstep, every sound, threatened danger. Since we had little or no access to news, people could only speculate, based on hearsay, about what might become of them from moment to moment.

From my perspective, things did not seem all that bad since I was living with my father. I believed deeply in him. It was almost like he had superpowers. I was sure that his love would save me from any and all jeopardy—simply because he was my father. After all, he had saved me before: first from the convent, and then from the orphanage. Besides, one day Father and I had a heart-to-heart talk. He told me that if, for some reason, we should ever become separated I should just close my eyes and visualize us being together again until he would surely return. He assured me that no Nazi could ever separate us. We would never be away from each other and that our love was eternal.

Father's suggestion did not come too soon, for the very next day, the Germans arrived and chased us all out into the streets of Budapest. Hundreds of Jews were herded like animals for miles along the cobbled streets. With our hands held high, we followed each other without knowing our destination. Finally, we arrived at the city's largest synagogue, where we were pushed through the doors and up the stairs; the bottom portion of the temple had already been filled with other victims. The place was so jam-packed that some people could not find seats and had to sit on the floor or remain standing. No one knew how long we would be held hostage or what our fate would be. The only thing we could do was to wait in abject silence. We had no food, no water, no toilets; all we had was each other. I thought of my mother, and again thanked God for having taken her before this horrible nightmare began.

The couple of days we spent in this inhuman confinement were just a prelude of what was to come. None of us spoke or befriended anyone, for fear of drawing attention to ourselves and risking our lives. Father and I were seated in the balcony area directly above the Torah, and as we looked down at one point in response to an agonizing scream, we could see a young woman giving birth to her child.

The day after our arrival, we had a visit from the high priest of Hungary himself, Cardinal Mindszenty. There was much excitement about his Holiness' arrival, since everyone believed that he was there to save us. But then, as he came to preach to us about the suffering of Christ, and how we must also bear the cross that was given to us, it soon became clear that he was simply performing an act. As he lifted his arms to give us his blessing, he exposed his gold-trimmed cape as if he was wearing the wings of angels. Finally he ended his performance by making the sign of the cross as a form of blessings on all the suffering Jews—which to the Jews was considered blasphemous. Following what he no doubt viewed as a noble gesture, he departed and left us to our unhappy fate. Some years later I learned that Cardinal Mindszenty was arrested shortly after the liberation, convicted of treason, and sentenced to life imprisonment.

Following his Holiness' visit, I was struck by a terrible stomach cramp. I told my father but all he could do was to comfort me, and hold me in his arms. We did not have toilet facilities and soon the place became a literal sewer. Two days later, dehydrated and half-starved, we were released and allowed to return to our over-crowded "homes" which, after a couple of days in the synagogue, seemed like a castle. Once back in our quarter, I discovered blood on my underwear which I learned was the reason for my pain. A kind lady told me that I had reached the age of womanhood. Although I was embarrassed to tell Father, I cuddled up to him, promising that I would love him forever.

The next day the Nazis returned with a vengeance. Bursting into our apartment building with guns and bayonets, they summoned only the boys and men who had to line up in the middle of the courtyard awaiting further commands, while the rest of us stood by helplessly watching our loved ones being herded away with bayonets jammed into their backs. I could hardly believe it. That my father, my heart and soul, my flesh and blood, was being treated in this shameful, inhuman manner! Didn't the Nazis know, could they not recognize, that this was *my father, my hero,* the man who had given me life? As I stood watching Father being forced to get into a truck that was parked in front the building, I saw him bravely turn to me, and wink at me one last time. And then the truck drove off.

His departure left me paralyzed, completely drained of life. I did not dare imagine the fate that was awaiting him—or me. The anger and hatred I felt for the Germans was immeasurable. Sobbing, I swore to myself that I would fight for my survival until my last breath—if for no other reason than for my father's sake.

Some people tried their best to comfort me, but it only lasted for a very short while, since none of us present was without loss and everyone was busy dealing with their own painful emotions. Besides, we were not given much time for self-pity. Before long, another battalion of Nazis arrived and chased us into the street, then herded us into a nearby park where we were made to stand in a circle, keeping our arms held high. This time their objective was to rob us of all our valuables, mainly jewelry, but even including gold teeth that were knocked out of people's mouths. I witnessed a very old man with snow-white hair being beaten to death with a club. Never will I forget his image, as he lay on the ground motionless, his white hair saturated in his blood.

For my part the only treasure I had was already taken from me— my father. Aside from that I had a gold ring with a ruby in it that my mother had made for me for my sixth birthday, and a thin gold chain with a medallion that represented faith, hope, and charity. Of course I also had my little gold-framed picture of Saint Thérèsa. Unwilling to surrender any of my precious possessions to the Nazis, I waited until the right moment, then quickly hid the necklace under my blouse, and just as quickly slipped the ring off my finger, dropped it on the ground, and kicked some sand over it to bury it. I told myself that after the war I would be back to retrieve it.

We stood at attention in the park for several hours. We were cold, hungry, and exhausted. Yet I could feel the adrenaline coursing through my body. When, finally, the sun began to set, casting the park into shadow, I decided to escape. Slowly edging my way through the crowd, I hid myself behind a tall figure, then, gathering all my courage, seized the first opportunity to slip away from the park into the street nearby. Then I ran. And I thought to myself how proud my father would be when I told him about the heroic gamble I took.

Since no one was brave enough to be out and about in Budapest day or night, not even the Christians, the streets were deserted. An eerie silence prevailed, occasionally interrupted by the staccato sound of gunshots, most likely, I thought, coming from the park. I was wearing my only pair of shoes, and all the clothes that I owned: a blouse, couple of sweaters, three pairs of underwear, two pairs of socks, my winter coat, two scarves, my hat, and a pair of gloves. I'd hidden my parents' photos under my blouse, and that gave me some sense of security. While walking as rapidly as I could, hoping not to seem suspicious or call attention to myself, I kept out of sight by staying as close to the wall as possible. Now and then, when I heard the slightest sound, I'd flatten my body against any object or hide in a crevice of a building, keeping as quiet as possible. I did not know where I was headed, but I continued moving away from the park, always on the lookout for an appropriate place to hide for the night.

Images of my father kept flashing in my mind. I kept using his name as my mantra, visualizing our reunion. I could hardly wait to recount the stories of my bravery and how I outsmarted the Germans, especially having dropped my ring and buried it for safety. I was very pleased with myself and was certain that he would be too.

As I continued to slither through dark passages, I thought about the past—about the days when my father and I spent fun times together—and then my thoughts became a game. Instead of fearing the here and now, I pretended that I was headed home to see family. That my walk in the dark was just a bad dream and that I would wake to find my father beside me. Then, suddenly, just as I was gaining confidence, I found myself face-to-face with a young Arrow Cross soldier who shouted: "Stop!" Removing the rifle from his shoulder, he pointed it right at me. I saw the swastika band around his arm and greeted him respectfully in German, quickly forcing a smile.

Even though I had not had much education, the one thing I knew well was the German language thanks to the German nanny I'd had when I was very young. Controlling my fear, I calmly asked the young man for directions both in German and in Hungarian, telling him that I was headed to my aunt's place and had gotten slightly disoriented in the dark. Luckily he bought my story, gave me directions, and let me go on my way—warning me to be careful and to stay indoors in the future.

Realizing that I was not a cat with nine lives, I knew that if I wanted to live I had to find some sort of shelter, and soon as possible. As luck would have it, I spotted some dim light coming from a basement. Taking a closer look I saw that it was a print shop but could see no one nearby. Hoping the owner would let me stay, I entered, ready with my sob story should he prove to be a Nazi sympathizer, but to my surprise the shop was empty. Not a person in sight. I quickly turned off the light, and carefully hid myself under one of the large printing machines, where I remained motionless till dawn.

The next morning I was awakened by heavy footsteps followed by German conversation. I curled my body into a ball and stayed hidden under the printing machine, controlling my every breath. The soldiers were searching for fugitives. They looked in the four corners of the shop, under and inside the large printing machines, but somehow they missed my curled-up body as it blended into the darkness of all those pipes. When they left at long last, I quickly retrieved Saint Thérèsa's picture out of my pocket, kissed it, and thanked her for her protection. Without moving from underneath the printing machine, I started calculating my next move. Where should I go? What should I do? How would I be able to escape from this hell? I was short of answers. One thing I knew for sure was not to stay in place for too long. Then, suddenly, I remembered hearing people talking about the Swedish protection houses. Rumor had it that there were several apartment buildings near the Danube that were under Swedish protection by law—which meant that the Germans were not permitted to harm those inside. This, I thought, was the perfect answer for me. I waited patiently till dark before leaving the print shop, then headed straight for the Swedish-protected housing. It was only about a half a mile away.

Luckily the doors were unlocked and I was able to enter the nearest building along my path. I was confident that my safety would be assured so long as I could convince the residents that I was one of them. Since there were so many folks living inside, no one knew who belonged to whom, making my task so much easier. Although food was scarce, I was able to get some through the kindness of the people there—all of whom shared what little they had. In a way, since we all had the same fears and suffered from the same persecution, we became a family.

Raoul Wallenberg, a Swedish diplomat, had begun distributing certificates of protection issued by the Swedish legation specifically to the wealthy Jews of Budapest. There were some thirty "safe houses" which together comprised a Jewish ghetto. Families who held these magical papers lived in the belief that short of moving to Sweden, their lives were saved, and that they were now living under the protection of a neutral country. Because these "protection certificates" were costly, many Jews were left out of the program.

During all this chaos, people were often separated from their loved ones. Many of them would spend their time reminiscing about the happy, peaceful times they had enjoyed before the war. They would often show me photographs of their lost loved ones, proclaiming their daughter or son or sister to be the dearest, smartest, prettiest ever born. At times like these, I listened with envy, my heart breaking—not for them, but for myself, for I knew that besides my father, there would never be anyone in the world, certainly not any of my other family members, who would ever carry photographs of me, or think such kind thoughts of me. At times like these, the possibility that I might never see my father again was too devastating to consider.

CHAPTER 7

Angels Pasture
AngyalfÔld

AS IT TURNED OUT, a certificate was no protection from those bloodthirsty killers who thought nothing of breaking the treaty.

After the horrific Danube massacre, I stayed hidden in the bushes till sundown. Then, when I finally dared to stand up, I looked over my shoulder and saw a line of pretty shoes, shoes that only hours before belonged to mothers, fathers, sisters, brothers— to people of all ages, who floated in what was now a river of blood. It struck me how fragile we were as humans. That one moment we were here on earth, breathing the same air, then the next, gone who knows where? Who knew what happened to us after life? I wondered if perhaps my mother was standing at the gates of heaven, welcoming those unfortunate victims. Could my mother have turned into an angel? In my mind that was possible.

Then, abruptly, I told myself to wipe the scene out of my mind and get on my way before I became a victim myself. Walking toward my grandfather's house, I desperately tried to erase from my memory the horrors I had just witnessed both in the Swedish-protected apartment building and by the Danube. Still, the sound of those desperate cries and the image of the shoes that were left behind kept haunting me, and they also confirmed the importance of my leaving the city.

Although by streetcar Angels Pasture was no more than a fifteen- to twenty-minute ride, on foot it took me several hours. But even though it was cold, adrenaline still flowed through me and I was almost too warm underneath my layers of clothing. My shoes were soaking wet from the snow and slush, but who had time to be concerned about things like that. At least I had shoes!

En route, I had to make several stops in order to hide from passersby as I did not want to be recognized as a fugitive, but I persevered and drew strength from the notion that under the circumstances my grandfather would surely welcome me even if he did not truly care for me.

Grandfather's place was not visible from the street. It was imbedded behind a long, narrow alleyway covered only by gravel and stones. In order to reach his apartment, one had to go past an old broken wooden door then walk about a half-mile along a gravel path before arriving at a small garden that surrounded a three-story apartment complex. Grandfather's small abode was located on the ground floor two doors past the outhouse.

As I walked along the gravel alley, I could feel my heart pounding in anticipation of seeing someone I knew—someone to whom I belonged, someone who was connected to my mother.

I envisioned telling him about my bravery and how cleverly I had cheated death. I believed that this time Grandfather would surely find me to be smart, and in fact would be proud of me. Surely this time he would love me at least a little, even though my reading was still not up to his standards. But when I finally reached his apartment, to my horror I found it boarded up with slats of wood; a yellow star was fixed to his door. The neighbor from down the hall reluctantly poked her head out and whispered, "The Arrow Cross dragged him out of his place about a week ago and shot him dead right out on the street. The poor man! We all felt so horrible!" Then she quickly closed her door, no doubt afraid that she'd be found out for giving out information.

In the early part of 1945, the Russians began to drop their bombs on Hungary. A curfew was immediately imposed on all citizens. Only during designated daylight hours were people allowed out on the streets. Windows had to be covered by blankets or sheets so that the lights would not attract enemy planes, and basements were converted into bomb shelters.

Germans, Hungarians, Russians—it made no difference. The seeds of hatred and prejudice had been planted, and they grew vigorously. Everyone lived in fear and suspicion. Love became an abstract thought, and every person lived for himself. Desperation and fear replaced honesty and self-respect. War was destroying the dignity of mankind.

Familiar with Grandfather's neighborhood, I decided to stay in Angels Pasture. Here I felt I could more easily maneuver from one hiding place to another. Besides, Angels Pasture was practically devoid of Jews, since the few who lived there before the occupation had already been assassinated. Naturally, I took steps to protect myself. First I changed my name, and then I made up a story that was fairly credible. Each day at 4 o'clock when the curfew began, and no one was allowed on the streets, I would enter one of the bomb shelters at random, introducing myself with a Christian-sounding name like Maria Nagy instead of Marika Roth. Then I would tell a story that went something like this: "I was on my way home, but unfortunately, I won't be able to make it before the curfew. May I stay overnight?" The residents felt obligated to keep me and share their food, at least until the following morning.

Being only twelve years old gave me a certain advantage, especially since my long pigtails made me look a lot younger. Depending on my particular need of the moment, I could pass myself off as either a child or a grownup. I was able to transform myself, not unlike a chameleon, without showing my fear of their possible suspicion.

As the Russians became aggressive in their mission to take over Hungary, bombings became fierce and almost nonstop. Residents were prohibited from visiting their upstairs lodgings or even coming out from their bomb shelters, no matter the time of day. People lived on a diet of boiled beans, peas, and potatoes, which they generally shared among themselves.

Each housing unit had its own patrol system. Every morning, a group of men was assigned to surface from underground to make their rounds of inspection on every floor, making sure that there were no Jewish fugitives hiding out in their houses. Relying on my sixth sense and with my faith in little Saint Thérèsa, I perfected my fake chronicle to the point where I could easily touch people's hearts with my sob story, and, for the most part, it worked wonderfully.

Naturally, there was the occasional glitch, like the time I took refuge in the house next to my grandfather's. That evening Grandfather's house was hit by a bomb and the wall between the two shelters had to be broken down, causing the tenants who knew me to move into my territory. I was forced to flee before I could be identified.

Then there was the time when in another house, I was made to share a narrow bed with the family's grandfather, an old man who because he walked with the help of a cane was considered harmless. Yet in the middle of the night, while everyone was sound asleep, this harmless old man suddenly found his youth, as he forcibly attempted to remove my underwear. Horrified, I jumped out of bed and spent the rest of the night wide awake, sitting up, praying for dawn to arrive. The next morning, when I complained to the family about what had happened, I was accused of lying and was promptly thrown into the street.

I had to move quickly and cautiously each and every day from one bomb shelter to the next, where I retold my fabricated story and gave my fake name. My system worked for weeks, and just as I was gaining confidence in my ability to survive, events took a sudden turn.

Late one late afternoon as I introduced myself in a new bomb shelter, I could tell almost at once that the people who listened did not fully buy my story. I heard one man say, "Those damn Jews multiply like rabbits. The more you kill, the faster they come back." Subsequently interrogated and cross-examined by a group of residents—a council of sorts—I knew that I was in trouble. But by the time I realized this, the evening curfew was in effect and it was too late for me to move on. Naively I thought I would be able to charm them as time went on, or at the very least slip away by morning, but things were not to go my way. As soon as the curfew was lifted, early the next day, the four-man team came to fetch me and escorted me out into the streets in the direction of the nearest police station. The men surrounded me as if I were a criminal, one man on each side of me and two behind.

We walked along the deserted street without saying a word, while all the time I kept looking for a chance to run. My heart was pounding so hard that I was sure everyone could hear it. *This is most certainly it,* I thought. *I've reached the end! There's no way out. This time I've walked into the spider's web. An inescapable trap that will almost certainly cost me my life! I will never see my father again.*

But even as we were nearing the police station, I was not ready to surrender. Just as we turned the corner, I saw a young policeman heading our way. That was it! This time it was do or die! Without the slightest hesitation, I bolted away from my captors and ran toward the policeman, to whom I excitedly poured out a fabricated story, pointing to the men who were still far behind me and saying that they were kind enough to try and help me out. Once the men saw that I was in the hands of the police, they were satisfied. They tipped their hats and headed back to their shelter, waving goodbye.

To my utter surprise this officer seemed kind and understanding—he seemed *human.* He assured me that he understood my dilemma and offered to take me to a shelter where, he promised, I would be comfortable and safe. He was young and friendly, so I was confident that once again good fortune had found me. We walked a mile or two before we reached a private house with a lovely picket fence around its snow-covered garden. The policeman had a key to the door, and we went inside.

The house was cold and dark. Sheets covered the windows, in accordance with the law, and the rooms—at least those that I saw—were poorly furnished. The policeman, whom I now thought of as my friend, introduced me to a man in his fifties who had a strange aura about him. He spoke in a whisper and his eyes shifted about in an unnerving way. Without ceremony he escorted me into the kitchen where he pointed to an army cot pushed against the wall and said it was set up for me to sleep on for the night. After shaking hands with the other man, the police officer tapped me on the head, smiled, and promised to come back the next morning to make sure I was well cared for while he was gone.

Since it was winter and I was a fugitive, I had learned to live in the clothes I was wearing, including several layers of underwear, tops, and socks at all times. I never took them off, not even when I went to bed at night. On my first night at this new shelter, the host of the house came to visit me while I was sound asleep. I was jolted awake by the touch of his cold hand under my blanket. It began stroking me in private places. Luckily, my layers of underwear protected me from direct contact. I shoved his hand aside and jumped out of the bed. Terrified, I stood awaiting his next attack, but strangely the man just turned around and quietly left me standing in the kitchen. After this incident I could not go back to sleep. Instead I spent the rest of the night sitting up, wakeful and afraid of my future.

In the morning, as soon as the policeman returned, I told him what had happened. Instead of replying sympathetically, he said that I should be grateful to be where I was, and that this kind old man had been hiding several Jews in his basement as his paying guests. The policeman reminded me that I was a non-paying customer. And then he unzipped his trousers, pulled out his erect penis, and demanded that I take it into my hand and hold it. I tried to get away but he grabbed me and held me firmly with one hand while he used his other hand to masturbate. I fought like a wild beast to free myself from his strong grip. Suddenly remembering my mother's instructions about self-defense, I managed to kick the policeman in the groin and when he doubled over from pain, he was forced to release his grip, giving me a chance to free myself. I bolted out of the house and ran as fast as my shaky legs could carry me, until my lungs felt like they might burst and I had to stop.

As I advanced along the deserted, snow-covered streets—some narrow, some wide—I kept thinking about my parents and how much I yearned for them. I was terribly frightened and lonely. It was November, the month that marked my thirteenth birthday, and it felt like I was hanging from a string not knowing where I was going to fall. Although I no longer believed in Santa Claus, I still believed in saints, and could not help but wonder if my mother could see me from heaven. I so desperately needed her help. And what about my father? Where was he on this cold winter day? Was he thinking about me, too? Everything I did, every step I took, was in hopes of seeing my father again, one day soon. Would we ever be reunited? I paused and closed my eyes as he had suggested I should, but I could not visualize his face.

While I kept walking on, every now and then visions of the policeman unzipping his trousers would appear in my head. I had never seen a penis before, and I could not comprehend that my father, the man I loved with all my heart, would be built in the same shocking way. By now I was mentally and physically exhausted. My legs refused to go any further, and since the sun was already setting, it was urgent that I find my next shelter right away.

All around me, bombs were falling, decimating buildings, one after the other. I could hear the bombs whistle past my head or, sometimes, from a distance. There were flames and choking dust everywhere. But my fatigue and depression erased all my fears. I was no longer afraid of death—only of people. All I wanted was to run as far away from that policeman as possible, and find shelter.

I came upon a four-story apartment complex. Bravely I climbed the twisted marble staircase to the top, and carefully walked around the balcony looking for an unlocked door.

Whereas earlier in the month bombings were more or less targeted at the smaller cities outside of Budapest, now the Russians were aggressively advancing toward the city and its suburbs as well. Bombings occurred at all hours day and night, and frightened citizens remained permanently in their shelters, not even surfacing for air. Certainly, living in an upstairs apartment would have been suicidal for them, but for me it was a refuge made in heaven.

I found an apartment that had a bedroom and a living room, with the kitchen located close to the front door. It looked like the tenants had packed up most of their belongings in a hurry. They had left behind only some silverware, a few plates, a pair of scissors, some cellophane paper, a pile of old newspapers. And a bag of dry, moldy bread. It was my salvation. As hungry as I was, the mold tasted like caviar. Although I was a trespasser and a fugitive, it was comforting to know that in this place I no longer had to put up with horrible men trying to take advantage of me, or with people who were suspicious of me. Nor did I have to lie about my identity. At last I was my own master.

It had been months since I had an opportunity to wash or clean myself. And my long thick pigtails, once a cherished source of pride to both my mother and myself, had become a torment. At first, there had been just an itch, but pretty soon I had discovered bugs crawling on my neck and forehead. Scratching caused my skin to bleed and scab, and the pus from the infection made my hair clump together. My scalp that was now infected emitted a terrible sour odor and I was burning up from fever. Finally I took the scissors that had been left in the kitchen drawer, laid the newspapers out on the table, and began cutting my hair to the very roots. I thought about my mother who so cherished my long pigtails, and how horrified she would be if she would have seen me at that moment. The world outside was silent just then, and I could actually hear the bugs fall onto the paper one by one. I watched them crawl around the old headlines announcing the coming of war and I cried.

War has a strange way of numbing one's feelings. I noticed that I had stopped worrying about material things, about my appearance, about what people thought of me. The only thing I cared about was the here and now, the exact moment in which I was living. I became much more in tune with my surroundings—I had to, in order to survive. And what mattered most to me was that someday soon my father and I would be reunited. Of course, I reflected, if I were to die, then so be it. I was tired and had lost my taste for life, anyway.

When I was done with the scissors, I rolled up the newspaper with my hair, and the bugs, in it, then shoved the entire package into the kitchen stove. Hoping no one would notice the smoke, I lit a match then stood by and watched with a kind of perverse pleasure the cremation of my little enemies. Finally I found a piece of cloth, perhaps an old dishcloth, which I wrapped around my head turban-style, then returned to the living room where I curled up on the floor in a corner. I felt relieved to have gotten rid of the bugs, although I felt terribly feverish from the infection. I sat and wondered, *How long will I have to live in this condition? How or will it ever end?* Then, suddenly, I noticed my shoes and how they had deteriorated over the months. All the wear and tear in the snow and slush had destroyed them. The soles were detached in places, and the laces were torn. Then I thought again of all the pretty shoes that were left by the Danube, and reminded myself that in a way, I was lucky.

Since some of the windows in the apartment were shattered from the impact of bombings nearby, and even though the place was freezing, in my feverish state I almost welcomed the cold air. Somehow, though, I managed to stay relatively warm by curling up like a cat in the farthest corner from the window, covering myself with all the newspapers I could gather.

One of the things that gave me some pleasure and distraction was the little shapes I cut out from the colored cellophane paper that was left behind. When I placed these figurines into the palm of my hand, they would move around and dance for me from the heat of my skin. Watching them was the closest I had come to joy in a very long time.

Because it was imperative that I stay alert and vigilant at all times, I was severely sleep-deprived. I did take catnaps, mostly due to my fever, but while awake, I indulged in my habitual daydreams by the hour.

CHAPTER 8

Liberation

DURING THIS TIME of seclusion, my vivid imagination became my primary tool for survival. I was able to escape from reality and transport myself to any place on the planet of my choosing at any given moment. Inspired by the movies I had seen with my father, one of my favorite places to go was America.

At other times I would reminisce about my happier days, when Mother and I went on our many outings. I think *La Traviata* was one of my mother's favorite operas. Perhaps it was because she could identify with Violetta who dies of tuberculosis in Act III. Mother and I loved the theaters, the fashionable restaurants, but most of all we both loved to window-shop and look at pretty shoes and dresses. I had to smile looking at my shoes now. Mother would surely have been flabbergasted if she saw my appalling condition. At the end of one of our days together, we would invariably go to a pastry shop, indulge in a slice of torte and hot chocolate, and rest our weary feet. Now sometimes I found myself humming the songs Mother taught me, and the familiar tunes gave me enough comfort so that I was able to doze off—all the while keeping one ear open, so to speak, for possible danger.

Often, my dreams were about my father. I recalled his joyful face when his horse came in first place, the movies we saw, his silly hat with the bird droppings. I remembered how hard we laughed the time his chair collapsed under him. But mainly I thought about how we just enjoyed being together being silly and having fun.

Memories of my past kept spinning around like a Ferris wheel. Many times I thought of my great-grandfather and the Victorian oil painting above his bed. How I envied those fortunate children who had no other worries but to chase each other around in that lovely garden filled with apple blossoms—happy, carefree children who had parents and no powerful enemies out to annihilate them! Often, I took my parents' pictures out from under my blouse just to kiss their faces.

But the vision that reoccurred most often was my future reunion with Father. I could actually feel the joy of his presence as he held me in his arms. I would become intoxicated by the aroma of his familiar tobacco—and allow myself to be deliriously happy just being a child again.

At the end of each day, and in celebration of my positive thoughts, I would reward myself with a single piece of dry, moldy bread that I had been carefully rationing since my arrival. Although the building's water supply had been shut off, I was able to extract a sip now and then from the tap, and having that, along with the moldy bread, made me feel very fortunate.

As I was unable to tell one day from the next, I had no idea how long I went on hiding in that apartment. All I knew was that one morning I suddenly heard shouting from the street below. Frightened, I dared to look out the window, and saw a large congregation of people waving their arms, dancing and shouting in jubilation right in the middle of the street. "The war is over! We are free!" My heart was pounding; I could hardly believe what I was hearing. I kept listening to their words over and over again, just to be sure. Was I dreaming? But then, as the street celebration intensified, I realized that what I heard was true. We were free at last! This of course meant that time had come for me to vacate my makeshift home and move on. The problem was, where was I to go next? What was I to do? How could I be certain that the Germans were gone? I listened and waited for what felt like the right moment to make my move. Finally, I wrapped each foot in a bunch of newspaper, tied it around with a cord, then grabbed the bag with the last of the moldy bread and slipped out the door. Even though the war *seemed* to be over, I ran down the stairs cautiously until I was able to meld into the jubilant crowd unnoticed, this time in plain daylight.

* * *

The Soviet Army occupied Hungary, more specifically Budapest, on Christmas Eve Day, December 24, 1944. Even though the war was over, celebration was premature. The Germans still held their positions, unwilling to surrender—at least in the outskirts of Budapest, which meant Angels Pasture. Consequently, the bloodshed continued, not just on the streets, but wherever German fugitives could be found hiding out. Even outdoor toilets were unsafe as Russian soldiers went on their killing spree. Just as the Nazis had slaughtered the Jews, now it was the Russians killing every German soldier they could find. I later learned that in the winter of 1944 when the Soviets seized Budapest, that event turned into one of the bloodiest of battles of World War II.

RUSSIAN AA GUNNERS IN BUDAPEST
CIVILIAN DEATH AND MASS RAPE

WHEN THE RUSSIANS FINALLY CLAIMED VICTORY, THEY INITIATED AN ORGY OF VIOLENCE, INCLUDING THEFT OF ANYTHING THEY COULD LAY THEIR HANDS ON, RANDOM EXECUTIONS, AND MASS RAPE. SOME 40,000 CIVILIANS WERE KILLED, WITH AN UNKNOWN NUMBER DYING FROM STARVATION AND DISEASES. DURING THE SIEGE AN ESTIMATED 50,000 WOMEN AND GIRLS WERE RAPED. HUNGARIAN GIRLS WERE KIDNAPPED AND TAKEN TO RED ARMY QUARTERS, WHERE THEY WERE IMPRISONED, REPEATEDLY RAPED AND SOMETIMES MURDERED. EVEN EMBASSY STAFF FROM NEUTRAL COUNTRIES WERE CAPTURED AND RAPED AS DOCUMENTED WHEN SOVIET SOLDIER ATTACKED THE SWEDISH LEGATION IN GERMANY.

Like bears after hibernation, citizens of Hungary gradually emerged from their hidden shelters deprived of light and food, and armed with boxes and sleighs, ready to vandalize the stores and make off with anything they could get their hands on. Before long, the once subdued, remote little town of Angels Pasture was suddenly transformed into a wild battlefield of sheer chaos. While people pushed and shoved each other, yelling like fierce beasts, I stood mesmerized by the madness, feeling ashamed of being human.

My immediate concern was my infected head. I was in desperate need of medical attention. Then I remembered that there was a hospital not too far away, so I headed in that direction. Luckily the hospital was operational. When I walked into the emergency room, to my horror I saw a young boy about ten years old bleeding profusely as his limp body lay across his mother's arms. His clothes and his skin were torn into bits and pieces and he seemed unconscious. I heard the boy's mother tell the doctor that the boy found a pen on the street and when he picked it up, it exploded in his hand. I later learned that the streets of Budapest were full of these boobytraps. Rumor had it that they were planted by the Russians; others claimed it was the Germans.

Rumors were mostly what people relied on during the war, since not everyone had access to radios or newspapers. Word went around that the Russian soldiers occupying our country were convicted criminals who had struck a bargain with their government to risk their lives on the front line in exchange for their freedom. This so-called liberation army was barbaric in its tactics. Just as the Hungarians were starved for food and warm clothes, the Russians were equally starved for women—and for all things that glittered and gleamed.

There were horror stories of rape and robbery everywhere, both in and outside of the city. Young women were captured and taken to the Russian base camp where they were systematically gang-raped and often murdered. Ironically, my good fortune was my deplorable smell and appearance. With my head bandaged into a turban, my feet wrapped in newspapers tied by strings, and my body covered with grime after months of neglect, I was pretty confident that no one, not even the Russians, would find me appealing. Besides, it was altogether difficult for anyone to detect my gender.

Since my grandfather's place had been bombed, ransacked, and shut down, I had no alternative but to head back to Budapest. Retracing my steps from previous months, I started my long journey to the big city on foot, all the while wondering if—and hoping that—my father would be waiting for me in the house where we got separated. All along the way, I saw many frozen corpses, half-covered with snow, spread all over the streets. I could not help but notice how peaceful and free from pain they looked once dead. It was almost enviable. On the other hand, horses that had been killed by bullets and now lay strewn across the road were like skeletons; half-starved human vultures had quickly dissected their bodies and taken the meat home for food.

As I was nearing Budapest, an army of Cossacks in colorful uniforms and fur hats rode past me on their galloping horses. They were shouting Russian declarations of victory, waving their swords in the air in triumphant jubilance.

When I finally arrived back in the capital, I was shocked to discover that my city was no longer the same place that I remembered. Underneath the gray skies and the snow-covered deserted streets lay hundreds of frozen dead bodies, a mixture of civilians and soldiers. Some were young, some old, some Jews, some Christian. One thing was evident—death had come to everyone regardless of their religious faith or national origin. This once magnificent, romantic city by the Danube had been transformed into a giant cemetery. It felt as though I were glimpsing a corner of hell.

Building after building was either destroyed by bombs or riddled with bullet holes. A park I passed was used as a dumping ground for hundreds of corpses ready to be forked into a truck and carried off for cremation. As it was around the end of winter, the snow and ice had begun to melt, and so had the bodies; the stench was overwhelming. It was hard not to vomit. I began running to get away from the foul odor, but distance alone couldn't erase the horrifying images, Trying to make myself feel better, I kept thinking only about reuniting with my father. I hoped so badly for news of him.

* * *

When, at last, I arrived at the house where we once stayed, I was relieved to find it was still intact and that the yellow star had been removed from the front entrance. As I approached the apartment I was so excited that I feared my heart would jump out of my body. Finally, I knocked on the familiar door then stood and waited for what seemed like an eternity before an elderly woman answered. I did not recognize her, nor did she know who my father was. She said she had never heard of him, but she did recommend going to see a family living upstairs that might have the information I was seeking.

I took the stairs two at a time and knocked heavily on the door. The family welcomed me warmly and even invited me into their home. They fed me and were very kind. It was comforting to be at last amongst my own people who accepted me for who I was. I no longer needed to hide my identity. However, the news they had of my father was unacceptable. According to their information my father had been transported to a concentration camp called Bergen-Belsen, in Germany, where although they assured me he survived until liberation, at the very end he died of diphtheria.

Survivalist that I had become, I flatly refused to accept their story. In my heart of hearts, I believed in my father's promise: that he would return. With my image of him planted firmly in mind, I continued my search. I went to Mrs. Kalamar, only to find that she had been killed and her place ransacked. Then I visited several of the coffeehouses where Father had been well known, but now I could find no one who could even remotely remember him.

I also visited the park were I was once held hostage, and looked for the gold ring I dropped and covered with sand. But the snow, the ice, and the rain had washed it away, into the invisible past. Nevertheless, knowing that at the very least I hadn't just handed it over to the Nazis was enough to satisfy me.

My next step was to visit my father's relatives, his sister Bella and his brother Miklos, who miraculously survived. But alas, they had no idea of my father's whereabouts, nor did they offer me any assistance. In their minds I was still a germ carrier, the offspring of a mother who had died of tuberculosis. Although they welcomed me as a visitor, they did not offer their extended hospitality—perhaps out of fear of jeopardizing their own lives. Oddly enough, no one seemed concerned about my appearance, or the fact that I walked about with newspaper wrappings on my feet.

One day I heard that thousands of deported Jews were being shipped back by train to Budapest from the different concentration camps and that their names were posted at the train station. This was the news I had been waiting for. I wasted no time in getting to the train station where I fought my way through the crowd in order to read the lists of names pasted on the cement wall right next to the entrance. There were two sorts of lists: first was a long list of those who survived, and the second was an even longer list of those who had not. I refused to look through the latter. Day after day, I went to the train station and read through the survival list, spending hours to read every name—never giving up hope of finding my father's name among them.

Later I was to learn that out of the 725,000 Hungarian Jews who had been transported to concentration camps, only about 260,000 survived. Most of these survivors had been from Budapest.

* * *

One afternoon, as I was pushing my way through the crowd, a well-dressed young woman approached me. Everything about her was perfect: her hair, her clothes, her shoes were of the latest fashion. Smiling, she said, "Hi, my name is Panny. Don't you recognize me?"

"No." I shook my head in awe. "Am I supposed to know you?"

She laughed out loud. "Why, of course! We were at the orphanage together! Don't you remember? I was one of the older girls."

To my shame, I had no recollection of Panny at all. Here was a girl only a couple of years older than me, and unlike me who was emaciated, bald, and wearing rags, she was dressed in the height of fashion and looking totally affluent!

Although I felt terribly self-conscious and uncomfortable around her, we did spend some time exchanging survival stories of the war. Panny boasted that she had found the secret for a prosperous life: by offering her special affection to men, mostly soldiers, in exchange for money. She proudly explained that her success was due to her talent as an entertainer to the many soldiers she befriended for the duration of the war, and that in fact those soldiers protected her during the invasion. Panny actually seemed to regard her services as an admirable contribution to lonely men in time of war. She later confessed that she visited the train station for one reason only. She was on the lookout for desperate men in search of their wives or other family members.

Seeing my deplorable appearance, she naturally knew I was in desperate need for help, and she immediately tried to persuade me to join her profession. But when she saw that I was appalled by the very suggestion, she eventually retreated. I told Panny I was waiting for my father and quickly bade her farewell.

The next day Panny returned and this time she insisted on helping me with no strings attached. She assured me that since we were both orphans, she was ready and willing to give me a hand. She offered to take me home to her place, which she shared with an old woman. Since I had no other place to go, I dutifully, yet apprehensively, followed Panny onto the streetcar. We travelled for about half an hour out of the city to a very working-class suburb.

CHAPTER 9

Panny and the Tailor

PANNY LED ME INTO a run-down housing development that had more the appearance of a motel than an apartment complex. It was even seedier than the place where my grandfather had lived. Panny opened the front door, which led into a small, narrow kitchen where a heavyset elderly woman sat drinking her coffee. After introducing us, Panny told the woman that I needed a place to stay, and that she would take care of my rent so long as she accepted me as her new tenant. Without further ado, the woman showed me into the only other room in the house. In it were two beds and one small cot. There was also one small closet, which was not a problem for me since I had no clothes.

The woman pointed to the cot and said, "This will be yours." Then she heated up some water on the stove, poured it into a basin, and suggested that I wash myself before going to bed. When I was done, Panny gave me one of her nightgowns, and all three of us went to bed.

It had been so long since I had slept between sheets and a blanket. And how wonderful it was to be clean! I was most grateful to Panny that night. Before I fell asleep, I said my little prayer to Saint Thérèsa and asked her to send me my father back. Next morning when we awoke, I heard Panny guarantee our landlady my rent, assuring her that she would also get me a job so that I should soon become independent.

A rather large factory that manufactured uniforms for the Soviet army was in need of sewing operators. Panny had connections there. Since I was barely fourteen, I had to pretend to be fifteen to get hired. Fortunately, they were willing to train, and during my apprentice period I could work as a trimmer, cutting off the extra threads. It wasn't long before I was promoted to sewing machines, and quickly was able to learn the art of sewing trouser legs together in rapid fashion. Even though my tiny salary only paid for my bed and bit of food, I was very grateful to Panny for what she helped me accomplish.

It wasn't long before I became accustomed to my daily routine: get up early, walk to work, put in an eight- or ten-hour shift, then go back home. Although Panny was still a tenant, my landlady and I seldom saw her since she hardly ever slept home. On weekends, when I saved up enough for streetcar fare, I would ride into Budapest, go to the train station, and look for my father's name on the survivors list. I still refused to give up hope and did not have the courage to look at the list of casualties.

The snows of winter had melted and spring was gradually approaching. Now that I worked in the factory, I was able to upgrade my newspaper footwear with bits and pieces of cloth that were a lot warmer and better at protecting my feet from the rain and slush.

But on the day when Panny finally came home, announcing that she got herself her own apartment and was moving out, she looked down at my feet and cried out in disgust: "We need to take care of this!" She told me she knew just the person, a good friend of hers who, as a favor to her, would get me a decent pair of shoes, tailor-made at no cost.

My life at the factory, where most of the employees were women, was becoming an almost pleasant routine—particularly because I was the youngest employee and almost everyone liked me. Using leftover scraps of material from the factory, the women took pains to wrap my feet well enough for added comfort. I had forgotten that conversation with Panny about my footwear until one afternoon when I was on my way home from work. I was passing by a tailor's shop when suddenly Panny poked her head out the door. She greeted me smilingly, then pulled me inside. As usual, she looked fabulous and appeared to be in excellent spirits. Panny introduced me to the tailor: "This is my friend Bela," she said. A tall heavyset man with dark hair and a small moustache was grinning at me as if he were the cat and I the canary. Laughing, Panny mockingly pointed to my shabby foot coverings and pushed me into a chair.

Knowing Panny's profession, I was not at all comfortable with meeting her male acquaintance and even made an attempt to leave, but the tailor insisted on me staying in the chair. "Now don't be silly, girl," he said in a deep voice. "We're only trying to help you out." He then took my foot into his hands for measurements and, smiling, he promised me a brand-new pair of pretty custom-made shoes, which he said would be ready for pickup in a few days' time.

That night I went to bed feeling uneasy about the tailor, about

Panny, and about my life in general. I yearned desperately for my father's return. It had been months since we last saw each other. So much had happened since then. Would he even recognize me? I was after all no longer his little girl. I had grown up into a wounded but brave person. I had seen and met with death so many times that it was no longer shocking to me. Dead bodies were nothing to me now. I couldn't have cared less about having shoes instead of the newspaper wrappings; I was used to it. But the one thing I could never get used to was the memory of those shoes that had been lined up along the banks of the Danube.

Grateful that my father was not one of the Danube victims, I took little Saint Thérèsa out of my pocket and asked her again to save my father. I said a prayer for his safety, and for all those who were sacrificed in vain. Finally I thanked Saint Thérèsa and my mother for their continued protection and guidance, then, placing the picture next to me on my pillow, I went to sleep.

For the next couple of days, in an effort to avoid walking past the tailor's shop, I purposely used the opposite side of the street. A week went by, and I had almost forgotten the incident, when on my way home from work the tailor stepped out of his store and pulled me inside. He told me that my new shoes had just arrived. He pulled a pair out of a box and held them up for me to see. "See how pretty they are? They will look lovely on your feet." Then, abruptly, he pushed me into a chair, locked the door, and pulled down the shade. I tried to stand up, but he held me down. "Don't be stupid!" he snapped. He put the box on the floor, then unwrapped my feet and started massaging them. His big fat hands moved up my legs to my thighs. I stiffened and desperately tried to pull away and brush off his hands, but he restrained me. I began to struggle with all my might. I tried to kick him. But he was very tall and very strong.

Then I bit him which must have hurt for I saw blood pouring out of his arm, yet he did not loosen his powerful grip. He was like a wild beast that had caught his prey. It seemed to me that he was perversely enjoying my terrified resistance. Finally, exhausted, I could no longer fight him off. He pulled me off the chair and dragged me like a piece of rag behind the counter as I begged for his mercy. I cried uncontrollably while he tore off my underwear. I threatened him with my father's vengeance. I even invoked the authority of the police, but all my efforts were in vain, for in the end I lay on the floor helpless and half naked, while his huge torso lay on top of me. No amount of pleading, no awareness of the pain he was inflicting, made any difference to this heartless creature. In a matter of minutes, I was robbed of my virginity in exchange for a pair of shoes that I purposely left behind once he let me go. I never saw Panny again, but I have always wondered if she had made a devil's bargain—at my expense—with the tailor.

Upon my arrival home that night, my landlady took one look at me with my clothes torn and drenched in blood, and she understood my pitiful circumstances at once. Without a word exchanged between us, she heated up some water on the stove, washed my trembling body, and tucked me into bed with a hot cup of tea and an aspirin. As I lay sobbing, still shaking under the covers, the dear woman tried to comfort me by saying that the good Lord would take care of its sinners. But I did not believe her. As soon she was out of sight, I took out Saint Thérèsa's picture and tore it into little bits. I promised myself that one day I would make it to America and would have all the pretty shoes I wanted.

I was so shattered, physically and emotionally, that I was bedridden and could not report to work for several days. When at last I was able to return, the women in the factory—knowing, perhaps, what had happened—were very kind to me. One woman in particular, who had been almost maternal toward me, approached me to say that her daughter in Budapest just had a baby, and they needed a live-in baby-sitter. This would be salaried with room and board included. Would I be interested? Naturally I jumped at the chance, and so began my new career, this time in my hometown, in Budapest.

*   *   *

Gradually I began to comprehend and accept the fact that my father was never coming back.

I grieved for a long time in silence, not just for the loss of my father, but also for my solitary existence. All I had hoped for, all that had been driving me forward, was lost. Also lost were my purpose and my direction. My mother had been right when she held her gun in my face. I had no future to look forward to. No one cared about me. I wished she had taken me with her to heaven.

Yet now at least I had a baby to care for—someone who loved me and whom I loved in return. Living with this family gave me a sense of what it would be like to have a family of my own. I decided to pull my courage together, and begin again.

Winter had passed, the leaves on the trees started budding, and the freshness of spring instilled new hope in my heart. Where I had been accustomed to hearing the whistling sound of bombs dropping overhead, now I was listening to the joyful sounds of birds. The ominous yellow Stars of David had been removed from building doorways, along with the Nazi occupiers who had posted them there.

In the park, colorful spring flowers had replaced the mounds of corpses and the radio featured big bands such as Glenn Miller, Tommy Dorsey, and Artie Shaw and their lively American music, instead of a news flash about the next dreaded air attacks. With the invention of a new dance called the jitterbug, I began to take an interest in dancing.

For me music was wonderfully therapeutic, and helped me in my conscious effort to forget the atrocities of war. Slowly I began to feel more optimistic and hopeful. That is, until the Soviet government started to take over leadership of the country, and began imposing their Communist laws.

The day I found myself standing among hundreds of Hungarians at a compulsory political rally, forced to wave a Russian flag, I knew I had to move on. I was through living with people who had betrayed their own country during Hitlerism, and I was unwilling to live through another dictatorship. At that very moment, as I stood in the crowd listening to communistic propaganda, I made a decision that I would get out this godforsaken country. Once again, I vowed that somehow, one day, I was going to make it to America.

I heard through the grapevine that Zionist movements were forming all over the different parts of Budapest, and that Jewish boys and girls who were interested in fighting for Israel were encouraged to join. This meant being willing and able to become apprentices as soldiers to fight for Israel, the promised land. In exchange for this service, participants would be transported from Hungary to Israel at no cost. I quickly went to the nearest office to sign up. But before I joined, I had another important mission to fulfill, which was to bid my fair-weather family goodbye forever.

Even before the war, it was compulsory for all Hungarian citizens to register their home address at the city hall, as well as at the post office, so it was easy for me to find my grandmother's address. Just as I was nearing her place, I saw her walking in my direction and carrying grocery bags. Although we were both on the same side of the street, as soon as she spotted me, she crossed over to the other side and hurried into her house.

I was hurt by her rudeness, but not at all surprised. Her insulting manner made me all the more determined to face her one last time, just to tell her how much I hated her for being so mean to my mother. I darted after her and knocked on her door until she finally opened it. She greeted me with cold indifference and invited me inside, where I was introduced to her unfriendly boyfriend, who sat smoking a pipe and reading the paper. He didn't even look up. In face he never said a single word all the time I was there.

While I remained calm and composed, Grandmother seemed uncomfortable and nervous. She talked a mile a minute. She never once asked me about how I had survived the war. All she could do was talk about herself. She told me how her boyfriend, who was Catholic, had been able to hide her, along with Aunt Klari and her daughter Agi, in the countryside until the liberation. But she never once mentioned anything about the whereabouts of Klari's two sons.

It was much later in life that I learned from Aunt Klari's sons that when Aunt Klari had been widowed, she'd asked her new boyfriend to leave her two young sons in an orphanage. When the orphanage staff refused to take them in because of lack of space, the man simply left the boys on the doorstep and walked off. Following the war, the boys were transported to Cyprus, and ended up living in a kibbutz in Israel. Apparently Aunt Klari never really gave them much thought. She did write to them occasionally, but that was all. It was clear to me that Grandmother and Aunt Klari were of the same mold.

As I sat and listened to Grandmother's blabber, I kept wondering how it was possible that this horrid person was related to my beautiful mother. I could see no resemblance, either physically or mentally. They were worlds apart! It was no wonder that my poor mother had been so unhappy!

Night was coming on, and Grandmother finally offered me something to eat. While I was having a small meal, I told her about my plan to leave the country. She didn't respond. Instead she told me that she was concierge of the complex, a profession that was considered below middle-class and nothing to be proud of at that time. I instantly thought of my mother, who I was certain would not have been proud. Then, just as I was preparing to leave, Grandmother told me that she had access to all the apartments, and offered me one of the vacant units upstairs for the night. Since I had no particular place to go, I accepted.

Then, to my surprise, Grandmother showed me photos of the family, and even gave me some pictures of my mother and herself. It was not easy for me to sit and face this woman who had done so much harm to my mother, and who had robbed me of everything my mother owned, without the slightest consideration for my feelings. I was unwilling and unable to forgive her then, and never will until the day I die.

The apartment Grandmother lent me for the night had obviously been vacant for some time, perhaps since even before the war; there was no electricity and it was covered in spider webs and dust. Grandmother gave me a flashlight and left. All I could find was an old sofa under the living room window. I lay down for the night, tired and depressed, wondering how anyone could be as heartless as my mother's mother.

The sofa was old and its wires were sticking out in random places, causing me to toss and turn. Each time I woke my mind wandered off into thoughts of my past, present, and future, until finally I fell back to sleep again—praying for morning to come. Then, at dawn, I awoke with a terrible itch. It felt like my entire body was on fire! I jumped up, grabbed the flashlight to see what was the matter, and found myself covered from head to toe by an army of red bedbugs. Appalled, I quickly stripped myself naked, swiped the bugs off, and shook my clothes. Once dressed again, I ran from this hellish place out into the street, never looking back. That was the last I ever saw of that wretched woman, my grandmother.

* * *

My next attempt to say farewell was focused on my father's side of the family. Uncle Miklos, a mild-mannered man like my father, did not react upon hearing of my decision to join the Zionist movement; perhaps it was because he did not believe in it. But my cousin Vera cried as we said goodbye to each other.

Next, and last, I went to visit Aunt Bella who, as it turned out, was celebrating her son Tibor's return from a concentration camp. Her dining-room table was crowded with an assortment of food such as I had not seen since I was a little girl. Everyone had a story to tell about his or her survival during the occupation. When at last it was my turn, I stood up and simply blurted out, "I am going to America!"

My announcement was met with a tremendous burst of laughter. Stunned and shaky by this response, I held on to the chair in front of me. Just then my cousin Tibor, who was ten years older than me, came up behind me and furtively pressed himself against me. I could feel his penis. In my shock I quickly backed away, no doubt giving my relatives the impression that I was a naive idiot. Instead of receiving encouragement, I became a laughingstock and the victim of a perverted young man. All this made me even more determined never to return again. I promised myself that no matter what, the day would come when I would prove everyone wrong.

CHAPTER 10

The Zionists

HAVING SAID MY FAREWELLS to my miserable families, I headed straight to the Zionist organization and signed up to bear arms for Israel. There were fifteen of us teenagers, all casualties of the war, ready to embrace any prospect that looked remotely hopeful for our otherwise shaky future. Training was intense, and our daily existence was minimal and strict. Popular songs and dancing were forbidden, but the *hora*, a traditional Jewish dance, was part of our regular daily routine. We learned how to be soldiers, how to shoot guns, how to be aggressive or defensive as circumstances dictated.

There were several Zionist centers around town, and each location had to wait its turn for all their members to be equipped with fake passports. We were to leave Budapest as a group, not as individuals. However, when our group's turn came, we were only issued four passports and tickets. This meant we had two choices: we could keep our group intact, miss our turn, and wait for the next opportunity which might not even happen; or we could split up our group, send the first people ahead with the rest to follow when and if their turn came. To split up the group, they needed four volunteers who were willing to travel without supervision. A meeting was called, at which time we learned that our fake passports would take us through Germany, and from there, we would be transported to Israel.

Fearing such a long journey to the unknown without the camaraderie of our group, the majority voted against the split. But as far as I was concerned my desire to leave Hungary was stronger than my dedication to the group. So without hesitation I raised my hand as a volunteer, giving the false impression that I was a hero for saving at least part of the group's turn. Once I made my "valiant" offer, three of my closest friends—Magda, Katie, and Zsuzsi—opted to join me for our long travel into the unknown. Before our departure we were given a backpack with a change of clothes, a pair of boots, and a bit of cash that finally sent us on our way to Cyprus via Germany.

*   *   *

Our journey took us first to Vienna, Austria, where, upon transferring to the next train, we encountered difficulties with suspicious security guards. Here my fluent German helped me take the lead. I negotiated with the customs officer, making up a perfectly believable story about relatives in Germany. Luckily I prevailed and by the next day we arrived at our destination in Ulm, Germany, where a prearranged truck was already waiting.

We were taken to an old concentration camp that was now being put to use as a holding place for refugees. Hundreds of transients just like us and from different countries were already occupying the facilities. We were all waiting to be transported to our final destination of hope, Israel, the Holy Land.

I was barely past fifteen by the time we reached Ulm, Germany, and had long ago lost my childhood innocence. Instead of the young, delicate teenage girl I should have been, I had become a tough, cynical, arrogant, and at times even obnoxious street-smart tomboy. Afraid of no one, I would not let anyone or anything get in my way. As the captain of my little group, I insisted that mine had to be the final word, which made sense to me as the other three girls had long depended on me, anyway.

Our living quarters at the camp were horrendous. We slept on army cots in close proximity to people of every age and gender, most of whom had not bathed in ages. We were completely deprived of our privacy, even in the bathrooms. Soon after our arrival, we were exposed to the humiliating process of disinfection; our hair and bodies were sprayed with petroleum to avoid the spread of diseases. Everyone was assigned some form of chore. Mine was to peel hundreds of potatoes all day long. Potatoes were virtually the mainstay of our daily menu, except for the occasional beans or green peas we were served with one slice of bread per day as a special treat.

Peeling potatoes for hours on end allowed me much time to dream and fantasize in my usual manner. I imagined myself in America, or someplace equally wonderful, like that incredible garden in Great-grandfather's painting. I also wondered what would become of me in the future. What was I going to do with the rest of my life? One thing I was now sure of, I could not see myself as a soldier with a gun on my back. Instead, I dreamed of becoming someone other than myself—someone people would look up to and who my relatives would envy. I also thought about my parents a lot, wondering if they were watching over me. After all, now I had both of them up in heaven.

Most immigrants at the camp were from Poland, Romania, and Czechoslovakia; few were from Hungary. Some had money, some did not; my friends and I had nothing but our hope and courage. The fact that we were poor bothered me a lot less than having to be around the people at the camp. Many of them had been exposed to a great deal of abuse and tragedy. Since Poland had been occupied a lot sooner than Hungary, the suffering those people endured had long since robbed them of their dignity. Trapped in their insecurities, they formed a narcissistic society in which they thought nothing of stealing or withholding things from each other.

They were also complainers, whining continually over their past as though they were the only victims of the war, and fully expecting to be compensated for their suffering—past, present, and future—by getting preferential treatment, such as a pillow or extra blankets, or being served additional portions at dinner.

I had difficulty tolerating my surroundings, and could not see myself going to Israel only to live the rest of my life among these ill-fated folks. Besides, there was a lot of hearsay and speculation about the ship, the *Exodus*. Rumor had it that immigrants were not going to be taken to Israel as was originally planned, but rather deposited on some damned island, a detention camp in Cyprus, where thousands of hopeful immigrants would be forced to live in tents under dreadful conditions. I paid a lot of attention to these rumors and decided to find a way out.

The black market was rampant after World War II. All over Europe people were quick to find ways to buy, trade, and steal, then sell at inflated prices such things as cigarettes, nylon stockings, chocolates, alcohol, and fake passports. At our camp, we had our share of black marketers circulating around, multilingual young men who came to our camp to sell such items. When I learned that there were train tickets into France, I offered to buy four at any price—three for my friends and one for myself—to be paid promptly upon our arrival in Paris by my French uncle. I swore that although I had no money, my very wealthy uncle in Paris would meet us at the station with full payment. The gods must have been smiling on me, for although the men hesitated at first, in the end they bought my story and before long my three friends and I miraculously found ourselves on the train headed for Paris.

We were escorted by two of the young black marketers who were determined to get paid. They kept us under close watch, and at times were not above making certain physical advances—no doubt, as a form of added advance payment—although we never gave way to them. While I was fully aware of my culpability for ripping those men off, I was operating on the principle of the survival of the fittest; the war had taught me that it was every man for himself. After all, everyone knew that these men were selling stolen goods that they offered at escalated prices, so as far as I was concerned, I was only stealing from thieves.

CHAPTER 11

Paris

THE STORY I TOLD the black marketers was not entirely untrue, for Mother's brother George was in fact a citizen of France, although not a resident of Paris. He lived in Lille, located north of Paris—some hours by train. While Mother was convalescing she often wrote to him, asking him to look after me after her death; hoping he would comply, Mother made me memorize his address. After all these years I still remembered it. Still, when I persuaded the black marketers to let us go to France, I had no intention of asking my uncle for the money. I had little faith in any of my relatives, and certainly had no reason to believe that my uncle would want to come to my rescue.

As the crowded train neared France, my friends and I made a pact that we would shake off our captors at the first opportunity. When the train began to slow down, we knew we had to be approaching Paris. So one by one we made our way to the bathroom, and as soon as we were all together, we jumped off the still-moving train.

Aside from a few scrapes and bruises, we managed to escape, unnoticed.

* * *

It was strange finding ourselves on French soil. Although we did not know how far we were from the Paris train station, we didn't care. We were on top of the world. We felt good about ourselves, about our bravery, about our freedom, and about the prospect of seeing Paris! We were giddy, almost as if intoxicated. We could not stop laughing; we laughed at the thought of those two young men looking for us, we laughed at how we had tumbled and rolled on the ground as the train moved on. We laughed at everything, but mostly at my clowning: I made up fictitious French words, impersonated people we knew, pretended that I was a glamorous but drunk movie star who fell on her face. Our laughter was therapeutic. We forgot the past and didn't much care about the future. We really were intoxicated with our freedom!

Once we had gathered our wits about ourselves, we decided to simply follow the train track into Paris. It was a journey of several kilometers, and it was nighttime when we reached Paris at long last. Even though our feet were blistered and we were hungry and exhausted, all the discomfort dissipated at the sight of this magical city, where the street lights and buildings lit up like stars. We had not seen lights like that since the war started.

It was refreshing to see tall buildings without bullet holes, and shops that actually displayed food. And then there were the breathtaking views of the Eiffel Tower, the Arc de Triomphe, and so much more! Fatigued to the core, we stumbled upon a park where we collapsed on benches and took the time to reflect on our next move.

Together we looked back on what we had seen and done with enormous satisfaction. We no longer had to fear the Nazis or the fascists, or any other dictatorship and their compulsory political rallies. There were no more nasty, pushy people with whom we had to share our food and space, such as it was, inside a concentration camp, nor did we have to go on an exodus to fight in Israel.

Still, if we were to further survive the odds, we had to come up with a strategy that would take us to the next step. Not only were we penniless, but we couldn't even speak French. The realization of all the obstacles ahead only made us laugh. We found the challenges awaiting us exciting. What really mattered to us was that we had each other, we were *free,* we were *young,* and we were in *Paris* instead of Israel!

Then, as the evening turned into a cold night, and the city became eerily quiet, our fatigue and hunger became more intense. Sitting on a bench huddled up together for warmth, we could hear our stomachs growling, crying out for food. To lift our spirits, I got up to dance a solo, imitating a ballerina. Soon my friends joined me, and we ended up dancing the jitterbug. This is when I came up with my next plan. All we had to do was to act like delinquents, make a lot of noise to attract the police's attention. That would certainly cause us to be taken to jail at least for the night, where we would be properly fed and given beds! We thought our plan was simply brilliant! Thus we welcomed the arrival of the gendarme, who, instead of throwing us in jail, smilingly gave us an address for the immigration headquarters where, he indicated, we would get food.

Early the next morning, we discovered that the French government was most accommodating to war victims and was eager to help them, especially the younger generation, the orphans. There was a large office set up in Paris to serve immigrants like us and offer immediate support—such as meal tickets honored by certain restaurants, pocket money, specially assigned hotels—all paid for by the French welfare organization. They also offered job opportunities in some cases, provided we passed the interview process. During my interview, because I naively boasted about having an uncle living in Lille, they insisted on contacting him. Almost immediately after they reached Uncle George, I found myself being shipped off to Lille, having to leave Magda, Katie, and Zsuszi behind in Paris.

MAGDA, KATIE & ME IN THE MIDDLE ON THE BEACH
NEAR PARIS WITH MY HAIR GROWN BACK

I did not take lightly my separation from my friends, who after all these months had become like my sisters. As I mounted the train, we wept profusely, promised to write to each other, and vowed our eternal friendship. My tears continued to fall for the duration of my two-hour journey.

Since Uncle George and I were complete strangers, I had been instructed to wear a band around my coat sleeve so he could identify me. I was filled with apprehension as I got off the train and stood on the platform waiting. Then I heard a man's voice call out: "Marika?"

As I turned, I saw a middle-aged man, of medium height and wearing a dark suit, walking toward me. "I am your Uncle George," he said coldly. "Follow me." His voice and his attitude reminded me of the time Grandmother asked me to follow her when we left the orphanage for Mother's funeral. I picked up my little bag and followed my uncle with a heavy heart, already fearing my fate.

Like my grandmother, Uncle George was cold and distant. There were no smiles, no embraces, no sense of being welcomed to his home. Uncle George looked nothing like my mother, and bore no resemblance to anyone I knew in our family. Naturally, he spoke Hungarian, but since his wife and teenage son Norbert could only converse in French, this automatically limited our ability to communicate.

The family had a nice large two-bedroom apartment with a living room and a kitchen. As Uncle George and I rode the small wrought-iron elevator to the third floor, we stood in silence side by side. He never asked me anything about myself, and I was too sad to care. His introduction of me to my aunt and cousin was brief, and smiles were nonexistent. After showing me to a small bed positioned against the wall in the dining room that had been set up for me, I was invited to the kitchen for a meal. I learned that my aunt was a modiste, creating fine handmade hats to order, and that the dining room was only used to receive her clients for fittings. Accordingly, all meals were served in the kitchen.

Because language was a barrier, conversation was at a bare minimum. Uncle George turned on the radio during our meal so we could listen to music instead. It was the first time I had ever heard Edith Piaf's nasal rendition of "La Vie en Rose." Uncle George asked if I was familiar with the famous singer, and when I shook my head, he began inquiring about the level of my education. Disregarding my unfortunate past and the fact that I had been deprived of schooling due to the war, he quickly concluded that I was stupid, and not even worthy of being sent to school. Additionally, he disapproved of my name and insisted that it be changed from Marika to Marie, which he said was more French-sounding and more befitting to my current life.

Before Mother died, she gave me a gold chain with a medallion that symbolized faith, hope, and charity, and was painted red, white, and green, representing the colors of the Hungarian flag. I had worn it always, never taking it off. I even saved it from the Germans. However, when Uncle George saw me wearing it, he confiscated it on the basis that I was too lacking in intelligence to wear anything as valuable as a gold chain around my neck. It wasn't until many years later, after I called him and demanded its return, that Uncle George mailed me my medallion to Canada.

In addition to his low opinion of me, Uncle George was also afraid that I carried my mother's dangerous bacteria. Accordingly, he made it his business to separate me from his son, my cousin

Norbert, for fear that I would infect him, so he moved the boy to his mother-in-law's house. Consequently, my cousin and I never had a chance to get acquainted. Eventually, Uncle George came up with a plan that suited him best. He simply sent me to work in a factory where I labored all day, spending long hours sewing garments, just as I had done in Hungary right after the war. Claiming I was incapable and too young to handle money, he had arranged to have my salary made payable to his name.

What Uncle George failed to realize was that although I may have been lacking in formal education, I was far from stupid. I had street sense and I was a survivor. Since he had taken my wages, I felt perfectly justified in stealing my own money back to get the fare I needed for my return to Paris. A few months with Uncle George was more than enough. So one day, after studying the train schedule, I got up very early, took the money I needed from my aunt's cashbox, quietly unlocked the front door, and slipped out of the house unnoticed. After running all the way to the train station, I was able to catch the first train into Paris just in time. Free again! It wasn't long before my cherished friends and I were reunited.

The following day, when I presented myself at the welfare organization asking for assistance, I was flatly refused, due to a phone call from Uncle George. He had reported my escape, and since he proclaimed his willingness to take responsibility for me, his offer automatically disqualified me from receiving benefits. I was infuriated. He was hindering my survival. I begged for a chance at a rebuttal, but I knew it would take time before I could get a hearing. Desperately needing cash, I stole some blank checks off the counselor's desk. By forging a signature I got myself enough money to live on. I knew from all my past moral instruction that forging and stealing were wrong, but I felt that I had no choice. It was a matter of my survival.

A week or two went by before I was finally called in front of the council. This time, I effectively pleaded my case, describing my uncle's mistreatment, and was allowed to return to the immigration program. Good fortune smiled on me, and I was back in the saddle again! I was given a job—hand-sewing women's silk undergarments—that paid a fairly decent salary.

Now that I was back in action and amongst my friends, we celebrated by walking and talking along the beautiful streets of Paris. It was July, and the weather was in our favor as we sat on café terraces sipping cappuccino or hot chocolate. Naturally our favorite pastime was checking out the boys in tight pants. Sometimes when we heard the radio playing Marlene Dietrich's rendition of "Lilly Marlene" with that German accent of hers, we all cringed, not only because she reminded us of our past, but also because rumors had it that she was once a spy for the Germans.

Since we were all between fifteen and sixteen, with hormones raging and a heightened desire for romance, we would have been prime candidates for a life of easy virtue were it not for the fear of the consequences. We were foolish, yet still cautious. We lusted wildly after boys because we craved affection. To us, boys were the best things since sliced bread. Besides, we were in Paris in the spring! What could be more enchanting? There was no one in particular with whom I was madly in love. I was just simply in love with love! Certainly for me, the need was not a physical one, for that horrid experience with the tailor had left me with much apprehension. What I was lacking was the love of a man—the love of my father. More than anything, I needed male attention.

July 14th—Bastille Day—in Paris was one of the most exciting experiences we ever had. There were bands almost at every corner. People were dancing freely on the streets with anyone and everyone. It seemed like love was free and rampant! I had never seen such exhilaration!

All was well until we heard fireworks, and since to us fireworks sounded like gunshots, we cringed at the sound of it, and quickly returned to our quarters.

Being unsupervised and unattached, we were four free spirits living our lives however we chose. Often times we tried to speculate as to what possibilities lay ahead in our secret future. We had no parents to guide us, no restrictions, no obligations, no expectations. In fact we were left with the worry about moral responsibilities all to ourselves. If we made mistakes, we had no one to blame but ourselves!

There was of course no shortage of boys in Paris, especially at the immigration center which was a kind of watering hole for us. It was where we got meal tickets and money. It was easy to pick dates and choose any boy we wanted. We were perpetually burning with the desire to love and to be loved. If we didn't have anyone, we made it up. We pretended that we were madly in love and fantasized about our imaginary Prince Charmings.

Magda, Katie, and Zsuzsi all started dating before I did, and because they were in a constant state of heartbreak and despair, I decided to play the field instead of being tied down. Instead of having one boy I had many. I enjoyed being in control of my life. Although I was not particularly attractive, I was very flirtatious and invited all the attention I could get, even at the expense of breaking hearts.

What I may have lacked in appearance, I more than made up for as a spunky free spirit with a quick sense of humor—a combination of traits that seemed to attract boys like magic. I was also dedicated to playing hard to get. There was no kissing on a first date and any sort of intimacy was out of the question. Several of the girls who were not our close friends, but who were also in the immigration program, became pregnant, a prospect that truly frightened me. I could not see myself being tied down with a child, and would never have wanted to be in that predicament.

Soon thereafter came the adoption program, and we were all transported to Versailles, just outside of Paris, where we were placed in a lovely big house which served as a holding unit. Although we had not been assigned any sort of duties and were not expected to work, we were nevertheless subjected to psychological tests which were to evaluate our mental state. These tests contained questionnaires; comparisons of words and numbers; photographs of ugly faces, from which we needed to make selections to determine our capacity to make good judgments. Once we passed the tests, we then had to await the legal papers that allowed our transportation to Canada and subsequent adoption.

During the waiting period, my friends and I spent much of our time sitting in the gardens at the Chateau du Versailles daydreaming. My imagination took me back to the time when Louis XVI was married to Marie-Antoinette. I could envision their gala affairs, their walks in that magnificent garden—which reminded me of the garden in the painting above Great-grandfather's bed. It felt peaceful sitting there, and I often meditated, projecting thoughts of what I wanted for my future. More than anything, I wanted to belong to someone, someone who could love me—who really cared about me and for me alone. Short of that, I wanted to become someone special. Maybe a nun, or a jazz singer? In my youthful mind I just wanted to show my relatives that I had made it. I wanted to become the object of their envy.

In thinking about the movies I had seen with my father, I was still patterning myself after the image of Shirley Temple. She always came out a winner in the end because she was charming and kind. I believed that Americans were nice, not like the people in my own country who had betrayed their own, simply because of religious differences. In their cowardice, they must have assumed Hitler would reward them, whereas, ironically, many ended up dying from the same bullets as their Jewish countrymen. There was apparently no place for loyalty among the fascists. I had long lost any love I had for my country; I wanted to be an American more than anything, and decided that I would settle for nothing less.

Finally the day came when my friends and I were summoned into the immigration office for testing of our intelligence. As candidates for the adoption program, we were subjected to a series of questions to establish our mental health. Although Canada was not my ultimate goal, I was fully confident that once I was across the Atlantic Ocean, I could easily slip away from Canada into the United States. I was feverish with excitement.

When at last the day came for us to leave Paris, we were entrusted into the care of a young male teacher, whose function it was to see that we were properly transported and attended to during our entire journey. Our first stop was London, where we spent only one night, yet it was long enough for us to explore some local stores and admire the window displays with chocolates galore. It had been ages since we had seen so many chocolates and our mouths were watering!

We left London for Southhampton by train, where we finally encountered our liberator—the gigantic Cunard passenger ship, *Aquitania*, which was built in 1913, and served in both World Wars.

AQUITANIA—OUR TRANSPORT TO CANADA

CHAPTER 12

Our Voyage

ALTHOUGH IN THE PAST THE *AQUITANIA* had been used to transport soldiers, after the war it had been upgraded, and used to carry the wives and children of Canadian servicemen from England back to Canada, until we came along. After World War II, it began transporting war orphans. To say that we were excited to see this gigantic vessel close up would be a gross understatement. We had never seen such a thing in our lives!

While we waited to embark, we were joined by another group of war orphans from Belgium, who differed from our group on two accounts: they were fewer in number, and they carried only boys with them—a fact that greatly appealed to us girls.

As we stepped on board the ship, none of us could have predicted the impact that moment was to have on us. We could hardly comprehend the fact that we were about to sail across the Atlantic; we had never even seen an ocean till then. And to think that we were headed for a foreign land—to the great unknown—to face an intriguing new way of life, and meet people who not only did not speak our language, but who were also to become our adoptive parents. Actually, I never gave much thought to the adoption process except for the fact that by having been chosen, it allowed me to travel for free across the ocean toward a new life, a new beginning.

As the ship began to sail, my friends and I ran out on deck to watch the white foam of the waves. It suddenly struck us that at last we made it. We laughed hysterically, not because there was anything funny, but because we were both excited and nervous. We began singing in broken English: *"Gonna take a sentimental journey..."* until we started to taste the salt on our lips, and realized that we were actually quite a distance from the shore. To add to our delight, a flock of seagulls surrounded our vessel and followed us quite a long way, sending out weird sounds, as if to participate in our final farewell from Europe.

But as the ship kept advancing, our laughter came to an abrupt stop. I think we all realized that this was not just a game, that we had literally reached the point of no return. All at once my spirits sank as my thoughts drifted back to my father. What if he had somehow returned from the concentration camp and was, even now, searching the streets of Budapest for me? How would he ever know to find me—so far away from Hungary, from Europe? The joy I had felt turned to fear and panic. My heart heavy with guilt and trepidation, tears filled my eyes. My friends noticed my silence and quickly moved in to console me. I knew that this was a moment in our lives when we all shared the same joy, the same apprehension, the same fears and exhilaration. Putting our arms around each other gave us a shared sense of comfort. And we realized that it was time to leave our past behind forever.

Our teacher Paul, a young Canadian in his early thirties, was friendly and responsible. He made certain that we were given our daily English lessons, and that we did not misbehave in any manner. Our days were well structured. There were lessons in the morning, and recreation in the afternoon, allowing us plenty of opportunity to flirt with the boys and to get better acquainted.

Just as in Paris, my yearning to mean something to someone—to belong, to be held, kissed, and loved—remained a constant focus in my life. Since I had learned long ago that making people laugh at my expense endeared me to them, I clowned around a lot and acquired many friends. However, in time, I also learned that often my humor was misinterpreted, and it either offended some or made me appear like a fool who was not to be taken seriously. I recognized that I needed to change my modus operandi. So at times when laughter wasn't the right note to strike, I learned to shift my behavior and display the sort of kindness my screen idol Shirley Temple practiced.

Fortunately I had some degree of leadership quality to offer, even in my younger days. Oftentimes in the orphanage, my friends turned to me for strength and support. By thus fine-tuning my persona, I managed to maintain some level of popularity and receive affection from friends who served as my substitute family. On the ship there were three boys, Zoltan, Andrew, and Frank, who soon became part of our group. We had great fun exploring the vessel, learning English together, playing Ping-Pong, and enjoying the delicious meals that were served us three times daily. We had ten days of this fun, relaxed journey before we arrived in Halifax, where we learned that because of the limited number of adoptive parents available in Montreal some of us had to continue the voyage on to Winnipeg. Unfortunately my three girlfriends were destined for Winnipeg. We said our teary farewells at the dock, solemnly promising to write to each other and vowing that our friendship would last a lifetime. Then my new three "boy" friends and I mounted the train with the rest of our group and headed for Montreal.

OUR FIRST OUTING IN DOWNTOWN MONTREAL
FRANK, ME, ANDREW & ZOLTAN

CHAPTER 13

Montreal

PAUL STAYED WITH OUR GROUP destined for Montreal. He escorted us by train and bus to the heart of the city, where he deposited us in a private home that had been designated as temporary harbor for orphaned immigrants. As the bus drove through Montreal, we all marveled at its Paris-like charm. The jewel of Montreal's city parks is, without question, Mount Royal. This 101-hectare park occupies part of the mountain that lies in the midst of Montreal Island, and includes the highest spot in the city. We soon discovered that this magnificent entity was in fact within two blocks of our new home.

During the days that followed, we were totally enamored by the beauty of it all as we went exploring the city, and by downtown Saint Catherine Street in particular. While I was charmed by all the beautiful shops full of pretty shoes and dresses, the boys were elated with the American cars—Studebakers, Plymouths, Buicks, and Cadillacs—parked everywhere. To me, this was all a confirmation that my dream of America was not too far off. After all, those were American cars! Then there were the wonderful American movies. And the American musicians Glenn Miller, Tommy Dorsey, Artie Shaw—they all lived just across the border!

Still, for now I was pleased being in Canada. Not only was it close to my imagined paradise, but from what I'd seen, Canada also did have its appeal. Besides, this was a country that cared about us immigrants. We were glad to know that soon we would be with families who would take care of us.

The house we lived in for now could accommodate over twenty immigrant orphans. The bedrooms were upstairs; downstairs were the kitchen, dining room, and living room, which were used for meetings with our assigned counselors, and for welcoming the once-a-week "adopting visitors." That was when wealthy families would come in their big cars to choose their preferred orphan. Not unlike selecting a likely tomato, I thought.

Meanwhile, we were given spending money and a good deal of freedom to explore our surroundings. This allowed us to indulge in restaurant food and get acquainted with grapefruit, cherry pie, chocolate sodas, ice cream sundaes topped with bananas, and colored soft drinks. All these things were foreign to us, but one thing that really amused us were drugstores, where aside from medication, you could also buy shoes, socks, and seemingly everything else you wanted under the sun. We were used to drugstores only selling drugs in Europe.

Although I fully appreciated all the generosity that was bestowed upon us, I personally found the adoption process humiliating. As I sat and watched the "getting acquainted ceremony" over and over, I knew in my heart of hearts that I could never call a stranger

"Mother" or "Father," and that I was much too old to be anyone's child again. I was only sixteen, but the challenges I had faced in my life thus far had pushed me way beyond my years. I suspected that the kind folks who came around "shopping" for orphans could easily sense my resentment, for in the end no one wanted me. Nor did they want my three friends. We were leftovers. And that was fine by us. In lieu of adoption, the welfare agency eventually placed the three boys and me into foster homes.

The fact that I could not speak English hindered my educational opportunities. The few English words we learned while on board the *Aquitania* were hardly enough. So instead of sending me to school, the welfare office elected to find me a job. Since I could operate a sewing machine, I was sent to work in a factory sewing pockets onto men's shirts. It was piecework, and I was paid three cents a pocket. Working under dreary conditions, with dozens of noisy sewing machines and constant supervision, did not help my self-esteem. During these times, I applied my usual "mental" escape technique by going on my fantasy trips. I imagined myself being far away, somewhere in America, where legend had it that the streets were paved with gold. I promised myself to find a way to the "promised land" as soon as the first opportunity arose. Naturally, I asked my parents above to give me some guidance.

My three buddies had their own dreams. Andrew, a skinny little fellow with spectacles, came from a scholarly family and aimed to become a doctor. Zoltan had a bit of background in boxing and lifted weights; he was also a very talented graphic artist. Frank, on the other hand, had neither credentials nor ambition of any kind. Short in stature, he seemed vulnerable, like a lost soul. In fact, we all felt sorry for this troubled fifteen-year old, which is the only reason we allowed him to be part of our little group. The sad truth is, none of us really cared for him that much.

Being maternal by nature, and still inspired by Shirley Temple, I volunteered to take Frank under my protective wing. Trying to compensate for his tragic past—if his sob stories were to be believed—I hoped to give him the encouragement I thought would take him to the next level in his life. One night while my foster parents were out, Frank begged to see me at my house. He claimed to have been very depressed. Since my foster parents did not like me having boy visitors, I let him in with reluctance. We sat on the sofa talking about his past as usual, trying to figure how he could best heal his pain, when I saw him getting teary-eyed. Feeling empathy and compassion, I took him into my arms to comfort him, and it was then that he started kissing me. To avoid hurting his pride, I let him carry on to some extent at first, but by the time I tried pushing him away, he was not to be stopped. Before I realized what was happening to me, it was too late. Soon after I discovered that I had became the victim of the very thing I feared the most, being pregnant.

Since I had just turned sixteen, the welfare office insisted that they would take my baby away and give it up for adoption—a proposition that nearly broke my heart. I was outraged to think that they would even consider such a thing. This baby was after all a part of me! I had no other family! When I told them I would rather die than give up my baby, they arranged a small wedding ceremony for Frank and me, with only my foster parents and the welfare people in attendance.

By the time of my wedding day, I was four months pregnant and suffered from frequent morning sickness. I was also suffering from fear of this marriage. A lot of things troubled me about Frank, but one immediate, inconsequential concern was the fact that he was shorter than I was which meant having to wear an ugly pair of low-heeled shoes for my wedding. Of course there were many other more serious concerns, some of which I was much too young to be able to fully comprehend. Still, my sixth sense told me that I was headed for trouble. I even fainted just before we took our final vows. Yet what was I to do? I was carrying his child!

Following our brief ceremony, there was no honeymoon, only a small party put together by a charitable family who felt obliged to commemorate the event. Some people brought wedding gifts and for some reason they all gave me pillowcases. I received two dozen pillowcases and one tablecloth.

OUR WEDDING

Although pregnancy was not kind to me, the day my little girl was placed into my arms, I knew it had been worth all the suffering. Her little face, her tiny feet and hands were so precious to me. Never having had much of a childhood, my baby was the first doll I ever had. Naturally, I named her after my mother, Elizabeth, and held her in my arms for as long as I could, but the nurses kept taking her away to place her back in her crib. Even as I was leaving the hospital, I was not allowed to carry my darling baby until I was securely seated in the taxi.

Elizabeth, my pride and joy, was born less than six months after our wedding. About a year later, my lack of education concerning birth control resulted in another pregnancy. It was a difficult time; I could not keep my food down for over six months. But it was all worth it when I was blessed with yet another wonderful child, a wonderful, good-natured boy with lots of black hair. Although Frank and I had had no conflict about naming our daughter, we found ourselves seriously arguing about the name we were to give our son. I wanted to name him Joseph after my father, but Frank insisted on Harry; finally we compromised and named him Harry Joseph. Although I was less emotional with my second baby, due to my troubled marriage, the moment that little body was placed in my arms, he melted my heart.

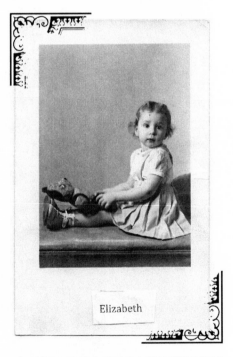

Elizabeth

ALWAYS THE LITTLE LADY WHO HAD TO HAVE THE COLORS OF HER CLOTHES MATCHING.

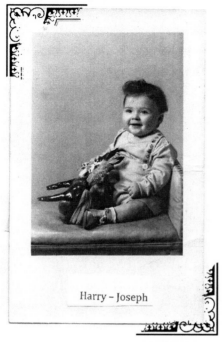

Harry – Joseph

WITH A HEAD FULL OF HAIR AND
THE CUTEST SMILE YOU EVER SAW,
EVEN THE NURSES FELL IN
LOVE WITH HIM.

By now I felt that I was a competent mother who knew everything about taking care of babies. There was a pediatric clinic nearby where we lived, and I never missed a visit to find out if my babies weighed enough, or too much, or if there was anything I should have done that I didn't do to better their health.

Frank, who worked as a welder/electrician, was not a good provider. He did not know how to appreciate family life, perhaps because he never had one, and it wasn't long before I discovered that he hadn't the least interest in raising a family. Whether it was due to his age or simply to his lack of character, he preferred to spend his money and time on cards rather than on his children. I guess he figured the welfare organization would take care of us.

However, by this time, the welfare organization fully expected us to start taking charge of our own lives. Because we were unable to afford an apartment of our own, we rented a room in an apartment located in a poor, working-class Jewish neighborhood, where the four of us were crammed into a single room. The old woman who rented us the space was very unkind, and she would only allow kitchen privileges to heat up the baby's milk bottles. Otherwise we had to be confined in our room. Meanwhile, Frank became an absentee father. Between his work and his outside interests, we saw less and less of him. Feeling very lonely, I tried keeping in contact with my two best friends, Andrew and Zoltan, but after I had married Frank, they both opted to distance themselves, unwilling to get involved. As for my girlfriends who went to reside in Winnipeg, I suppose the distance between us simply put an end to our relationship.

At times Frank would come home late at night, and at other times not at all. Then, when he did show up, he became increasingly hostile and even violent. He had a perverted need to show his manhood by slapping me around. Perhaps it was due to his small stature. Perhaps it was because of his inarticulate nature. At last, in desperation, I turned to the welfare office for help. I pleaded with them to help us be rid of Frank as our safety was jeopardized, and they took pity. They moved my babies and me into a rabbi's home—leaving Frank behind.

I must admit that the thought of moving into a rabbi's home gave me instant claustrophobia. As far as I was concerned, I had had enough of living with Jews in an enclosed area. In the aftermath of the war, after all that I'd been through, I had no desire to be identified as a Jewish person and could not foresee myself ever doing that again. But my options were limited. I could accept the offer from the welfare office, I could find accommodation on my own, or worse, I could stay with Frank. I opted to move in with the rabbi and his family.

As one would expect, at the rabbi's there were strict religious rules. No lights and no work on the Sabbath, milk had to be separated from meat and all foods had to be kosher—they had to have been blessed by a rabbi. Although I strongly objected to these old-fashioned traditions—all the restrictions, rules, regulations—I made it my business to try and respectfully overcome my distaste due to desperation.

In time, my children and I settled in and found the rabbi and his family to be very unlike the Jewish people I had learned to dislike in the past. These people were kind and gentle folks. Refined as they were, they had much love and appreciation for all mankind. They also loved classical music, and, in the evening while my babies were asleep, they would include me in their family gatherings. We would sit in the living room and listen to Mendelssohn's Violin Concerto, or Vivaldi's *Four Seasons,* or Bach, Mozart, or Beethoven. These special family moments elevated my soul and spirit. Learning about and listening to classical music allowed me to forget my miserable existence and offered me hope for the finer things in life, perhaps a better future. I knew that Mother would have approved.

Frank was not happy with our new arrangement. Now that we were settled elsewhere, suddenly he expressed an interest in being a part of our little family. Of course he first had to go through the welfare organization to get permission to visit. He would come with a litany of new promises. One time, he even brought me a large bouquet of roses as a peace offering. Later, I found out that he had put the charges on my bill, and I had to come up with the money to pay for them. Still, for a time, Frank did try to adjust with the intervention and guidance of the welfare office, and for the children's sake, we all decided to give him another chance.

Trusting in his sworn promises, I left the rabbi's home and we four moved into a small apartment. Since Frank did not bring in much money as a welder, I tried to think of ways to supplement our income. However, since my English was still quite limited and I had very little formal education, I was hard-pressed to find suitable jobs. Also, being the mother of two babies further hindered my possibilities.

It was obvious that all the cards were stacked against me. But then I came up with the idea of being a nightclub singer. Even with my poor English, I knew the lyrics to all the songs of Doris Day, Sarah Vaughan, and Ella Fitzgerald. I had been a successful choir singer at the orphanage; why not also in a nightclub? I spent hours practicing in front of the mirror until I built up my confidence. Then, leaving my babies with a neighbor, I headed to a club downtown for a tryout.

On my way to the club, I already had visions of my name in lights. Following a brief negotiation with the club's manager, I soon found myself standing on stage in front of a microphone. My tryout was to be in front of an audience! I was wearing a simple skirt and a blouse—the only decent clothes I owned. My long wavy hair fell to my shoulders, combed in the style of my new screen idol, Rita Hayworth. I could hardly breathe from excitement at the thought of singing on stage to an audience.

I whispered the title of my song, "They Try to Tell Us We're Too Young," to the pianist, struck a sex-kitten pose in front of the microphone, and waited for the music to start. Then the pianist leaned over to ask, "What key?"

Key? I didn't know what he was talking about. All I could do was shrug. His question completely threw me off guard and I panicked. But there was no time to waste as suddenly the stage lights were turned on me, blinding me. The pianist hit the first note. My hands were shaking and all I could do was to belt out my well-rehearsed song: *"They try to tell us we're too young…"* Although I did get some applause, it was no surprise that I wasn't asked for an encore.

My second attempt at professional singing occurred as a result of a small ad that caught my eye in the newspaper, announcing a contest at a park across town. Based on Mother's oft-repeated suggestion—"Believe in yourself"—I was determined to give it a try. I scraped together every penny I had to purchase a beautiful navy blue dress with white flowers and a petticoat and a pretty pair of navy blue shoes to match. Although the shoes didn't fit very well, I bought them anyway because I wanted to look perfect. As I dished out my last penny I did so thinking that this was after all an important investment what could be my lifelong career. Once again, I could almost see my name in lights when I looked into the mirror.

With all the confidence and hope in the world, and with the naiveté of a nineteen-year-old, I started on my journey across town, transferring from one streetcar to another, and then onto a series of buses. The trip took what seemed like forever. What's more, along the way, it started to sprinkle. Soon the sprinkles turned to rain, and finally it was pouring buckets as I stood waiting for my fifth transfer—without an umbrella. By the time I reached my destination, the navy dye from my dress was running down my legs and the material had shrunk badly, revealing the petticoat underneath.

Although I was cold, miserable, my feet had blistered, and I looked more like a clown than a star, I was resolute. I had come too far to turn back, and besides, I had invested all my money in this enterprise. At last I arrived at the park. It wasn't very large, so it was easy enough to spot the gathering of people. I was gasping with excitement as I made my final touchups to my botched appearance, then hurried on to join the crowd, only to find that the contest was for children between the ages of five and twelve.

I had made an absolute fool of myself. Humbled and heartbroken, I returned home, crying. I told myself that this was my last attempt at a singing career.

True to Frank's unkind nature, he had a good laugh over my unfortunate incident. After weeks of ridicule and abuse, he warned me to stay in my corner where I belonged, and to forget about finding a career. In his mind, I had no redeeming qualities as a mother or a singer and he was quick to tell me just that. Accustomed to his mean-spirited remarks, I refused to yield to his demands, and in spite of him—or because of him—I began looking for a different sort of career.

It was 1952; I was nearing my twenty-first birthday, and had spent the past three years of my life practically locked behind doors with my two children, but without a true husband and without friends. I was a prisoner of my own making and I hated myself for my mistake. As much as I loved my children, I felt terribly lonely and isolated. I was living with a man who gave me no love and no hope for the future. The deprivation made me burn all the more with a desire to make something of myself. I needed attention. Music had always been my passion, and although I had given up on the idea of becoming the next Doris Day or Sarah Vaughan, I still maintained hope of becoming something or somebody— maybe a ballroom dancer? I felt I had some talent, and the mirror was my best teacher. Since I had such great love for music I spent hours dancing with my children or alone to the music on the radio.

There were two large popular dance schools located on Saint Catherine Street, the main street in Montreal. One was named Rosita & Deno and the other was a Fred Astaire school. Since these two studios were in constant competition with each other, Mr. and Mrs. Deno, a Latin American couple, were always out scouting for promising talent. I went and auditioned, and to my utmost delight, they actually hired me.

Mr. and Mrs. Deno recognized my talent and took me under their personal wings for training. This meant many rehearsals and practice hours, which caused me to get promoted to be one of their top performers at the competitions with other dance studios. For the first time in my life, I truly felt accomplished. I was now earning a living doing something I truly loved—something that elevated my confidence.

But all was not well at home, for Frank had become jealous of my success. One afternoon while I was in the midst of giving a mambo lesson to a student, he barged into the studio, pulled me off the dance floor, slapped my face in front of everyone, then shoved me down the stairs—all the while calling me a slut, a whore, an unfit mother. Shortly after this violent incident, Mr. Deno informed me that he no longer needed my services, for after all he had his studio's reputation to consider.

It became very clear that to save my soul, and even my life, I needed to distance myself as well my children from this madman. With one phone call to a friend who was a stay-at-home mom, I was able to secure the three of us a new place to stay. My friend, who needed extra income, was more than happy to rent us a room, as well as look after my babies while I searched for employment. Without a moment's hesitation I packed our bags and moved us out of our apartment without leaving Frank a note.

Since I was hard-pressed for money, I was prepared to take any job that came my way. By now, my English had improved and I was able to converse more easily. Fortune smiled on me, and I was hired as a waitress at the Ritz-Carlton, one of the most prestigious hotels in Montreal.

My new life quickly settled into a pleasant routine. I worked the day shifts, which enabled me to be with and to take care of Elizabeth and Harry in the evening. Once in a while I indulged in a brief outing with my new friend Karen Tozer, another waitress who worked my shift.

Karen was British, from the Guernsey Islands. She had an air about of her that British "stiff upper lip" quality that I absolutely loved. She was the sort of person who chose her friends very cautiously, and the fact that she accepted me was good for my ego. I admired Karen's beauty and the European elegance that came as second nature to her. We were the same age, and had many of the same interests.

A couple of months went by without any news or disturbance from Frank, and I was beginning to feel comfortable in my fool's paradise—thinking that all was well. In my youthful innocence I never suspected it was possible for the worst yet to come.

Frank suddenly resurfaced, this time with a vengeance. He did not come to me face-to-face but rather as a stalker, no doubt with the intention of intimidating me. Day after day, he followed me; at night I could feel his presence behind me. He would stand for hours on the opposite side of the street from my window. It was most unnerving. It was like a dark cloud hanging over my head. In short, Frank became my personal Nazi. He was someone

I feared just as much for I knew that in his sick mind he was capable of anything.

From the time I started dodging Frank, it felt very much like being back in the war, when I was a fugitive. Once again I had to be constantly vigilant. If I didn't hate Frank before, I most certainly hated him now, not just for threatening and pursuing us but also for forcing me to relive my dreadful past. Whereas before I only had myself to worry about, now I had my little family, my two children who meant more to me than life itself.

While I rather liked my work at the Ritz since it offered several benefits—decent tips, a chance to make friends, and the sort of upper-class clientele that reminded me of my early childhood— to me the best benefit was meeting Karen. She was the product of a broken home, and therefore understood my dilemma and supported me with great kindness and sympathy.

Meanwhile, unbeknownst to me, Frank had been concocting a dreadful plan. Following his weeks of pursuit, one evening he finally decided to take further action. I was putting my children to bed, when suddenly he burst into the house, darted up the stairs, pushed open the front door, and charged into our room wielding a knife.

To me, this was a reenactment of the time the Germans swarmed into the apartment building and killed everyone on the balcony. Luckily, both my motherly instinct and my past experience with violence gave me the strength to confront this madman without backing off. Since I had my baby son in my arms, I quickly placed him in his crib then covered both him and Elizabeth with a blanket, and stood protectively in front of them. "What the hell do you want?" I snapped bravely, trying not to show my fear.

Frank's face was drained of color as he slowly advanced toward me holding the knife. He slapped me across my face, then pressed the knife to my throat. "You whore!" he shouted. "I'll never let you have *my* kids. You're an unfit mother!"

I shoved his knife to the side, and a terrible struggle began. I pushed him away and he staggered backwards, but he quickly recovered and pressed the cold steel of the knife against my throat again. "You're crazy!" I shouted, then cried out, "Help!" Fortunately, within seconds, my friend and her husband came running. My friend's husband, who was at least a head taller than Frank, grabbed him by the arm, pushed him down the stairs, and threw him into the street, yelling after him, "Don't you ever show your face in this house again or I'll call the police!" Afterwards my friend did call the police but by the time they arrived, there was no trace of Frank. He had vanished into the darkness of the night, leaving behind an enduring sense of fear and countless sleepless nights thereafter.

Following the policemen's questioning, I realized I would not be getting protection, since Frank took the knife with him when he left and my witnesses were not considered credible, since they were my close friends. In addition, technically, I was classified as a kidnapper for I had moved my children away from Frank without obtaining legal rights or providing some sort of notice. Another strike against me was the law in Quebec, which in the fifties favored fathers in custody battles. I felt that I was left with but one choice, which was to move from Montreal to Toronto, Ontario, where I foresaw a more promising future.

The idea of going with us to Toronto appealed to Karen immensely since, being British, she saw Toronto as much more British-oriented than Montreal. This was the beginning of the separatist movement period, when the Parti Quebecois campaigned strongly to make French the official language of their province. It was our good fortune that Karen already knew of an address in Toronto where we could stay, which made our transition that much easier. So I quickly packed up and, without leaving a forwarding address, Karen and I said goodbye to our jobs, our friends, and to Montreal, then the four of us boarded a train to Toronto.

We arrived with very little luggage, and hardly any clothes. There was just enough money to hold us until we hopefully found employment, which according to our calculation would have to be soon. Our new landlady was a single mother with a grown son called Bob, who was most accommodating. While the landlady watched my Elizabeth and Harry—now ages three and four—Bob acted as our tour guide to help us get acquainted with the city.

Bob was in his mid-twenties, like us. He was over six feet tall, soft-spoken, with a pleasant personality—the sort of man I took to very easily. Sensing my interest, he was all the more obliging when it came to helping me find someone to look after my children while I worked. It wasn't long before he introduced me to a couple whose business it was to look after toddlers full-time, which allowed me to search for a waitressing job. I did find a position but it meant working late into the evening and being with the children during the early part of the day; my choices were limited and I was glad to have a job at all. When more than a month had gone by without incident regarding Frank, I was beginning to feel less frightened and more confident. After all, I figured, since we had moved to a new city without leaving a forwarding address, there was no way that Frank could ever find us.

With my excellent reference from the Ritz, I soon found work waiting on tables at the Town and Country, one of the best club/restaurants in Toronto. Here people dined amidst white tablecloths and candlelight, drank champagne, and listened to high-profile jazz musicians such as Art Tatum, Oscar Peterson and his trio, Louis Armstrong, Marian McFarland, Ahmad Jamal, and Dizzy Gillespie. Working near such jazz greats inspired me to fall in love with their music forever.

Karen found work in an office, and soon our lives began to take form, allowing us to settle into a comfortable routine. I would spend time with my children before or after work daily, then stop off for a cup of coffee or a bite to eat with Bob and/or Karen at a nearby restaurant which was pretty much the extent of my recreation.

One day, while Bob and I were sitting by the window in a restaurant near where we lived, sipping our coffee, I suddenly had this strange sensation, like a premonition mixed with fear. My neck stiffened from nerves and as I started massaging it I saw someone staring at me through the window. To my horror, I recognized him at once—it was Frank! "Oh my God!" I exclaimed, gasping for air.

Bob was shocked. "What? What's the matter? You look like someone who'd seen a ghost!"

I could hardly swallow as I answered, "I did! I just saw my husband! He's standing outside!" Before I could utter the next word Frank was already standing by our table.

Uncharacteristically he appeared calm and collected, in control of his emotions—at least on the surface. He spoke in a very low tone voice, asking, almost pleading, to see the children. With an obviously fake smile on his face he added, "You know, of course, that it's my legal right. If you refuse I can have you arrested and thrown in jail for kidnapping."

Feeling trapped, I told him I understood, and gave him the address of the children's sitters.

The next morning I called the sitters to let them know about Frank's upcoming visit. They told me they knew all about it, for Frank had already been there. The next day Frank returned to the sitters' place. This time he wanted more than just a visit. He wanted to take Harry and Elizabeth out for a short walk. The sitter called me to ask my permission. Mindful of my lack of legal rights, I reluctantly consented. And that was the last I saw of my children until they were eleven and twelve.

CHAPTER 14

Kidnapping

⟨⟨⟨⟨⟨⟨⟨⟨⟨⟨⟨⟨⟨⟨

THERE WERE SIMPLY NO WORDS to describe my deep sense of loss when I discovered my children missing. I felt a terrible guilt for my inadequacy as a mother and I kept blaming myself for everything, all the while hearing Frank's echoing words: "You're an unfit mother." Maybe Frank was right. Maybe I just didn't deserve to have my children. But then, what was I without them in my life? I had nothing and no one else. Overcome by a feeling of worthlessness, I fell into a deep depression.

Naturally I made every conceivable effort to locate my little family. I called the police and hired a lawyer, but no one was able to supply me with any information. No amount of tears, no amount of pleading could bring my children back again. They had simply vanished. When I begged with my lawyer to try harder, telling him that I saw no point in continuing my life without them, his response was: "Don't you worry, your husband will bring them back before long. After all, how could he possibly take care of them?"

MY CHILDREN BEFORE THE KIDNAPPING

THE SITTER'S HOUSE IN TORONTO FROM
WHERE THE CHILDREN WERE TAKEN

Both Karen and Bob tried their best to console me, but their efforts were wasted. I felt like a dead person walking, an empty shell. The absence of my children was very much like the loss of my parents. Along with the insurmountable guilt, I was overwhelmed by concern for their safety and well-being. Every time I saw a mother with a child, I cried. Every time I saw a baby, I cried. I cried for months, always, oddly enough, recalling what my mother would say to me whenever she found me crying. "Crying is good for you, my dear. It empties your brain of all that excess water."

ME WITH CHILDREN BEFORE THE KIDNAPPING

I would spend hours in church staring at the crucifixion, identifying with the pain Jesus must have felt. On a daily basis I called the lawyer, who only said, "Don't worry, your children will turn up." But months went by, and still there was no news of them. Short of killing myself, which was a serious consideration, Karen urged me to keep praying and be patient. She assured me that in time God would hear me and some form of miracle would return my little family to me. I decided Karen had to be right and that instead of crying and feeling sorry for myself I should make use of this time to improve myself.

Karen suggested that I go to school, study, read, get some education—so that when I did get my children back, I would be the

MY FRIEND KAREN TOZER

best mother I could be for them. So with Karen's encouragement I began to read and study. I wanted Elizabeth and Harry to be proud of me.

Suddenly my project to educate myself gave me something on which to hang my hopes. Not knowing where to start, I spent hours in the university library observing which materials the students were reading, and I tried duplicating their regimen. All at once I developed a tremendous thirst for knowledge—I wanted to learn and know everything. I bought and read as many books as I could—by François DeMauriac, Dostoyevsky, Balzac, Tolstoy, Steinbeck, Voltaire, Flaubert, Dickens, Freud. I studied mythology; I read as many books I could on psychology. I envied the students who had a chance to study in college, and oftentimes I just sat in the library pretending that I was one of them.

Karen and I moved from Bob's house to a nicer neighborhood. My brief relationship with Bob ended on a sour note when I discovered that he had a serious drinking problem. I could never tolerate drunkenness. Our new abode was located in an upscale neighborhood; it was closer to the university, which was a big benefit to me. Much of my free time was spent on the campus.

Karen's ambition was more focused on her looks. Although she never made a big deal about her natural beauty, she knew she possessed that special something and was determined to pursue a career as a model. While I busied my brain with scholarly studies, Karen elected to further enhance her appearance by signing up for a modeling course.

I have always admired good looks. Perhaps this was due to my mother, who I thought was the most beautiful person I ever knew. During the time Karen and I were friends, I became used to men gravitating toward Karen, and if unsuccessful they would often use me as bait to get to know her. I did not mind my minor role, as it made me feel useful, and I had never thought of myself as even remotely attractive anyway, particularly in comparison to Karen. Besides, the fact that Frank never missed a chance to tell me how unattractive I was, with my long skinny legs and buck-teeth, stayed with me, for at the time I believed him.

When Karen approached me with the idea of signing up with her at the Walter Thornton Modeling Agency, the most prestigious modeling school in Ontario, I laughed at the absurdity of her suggestion. But Karen was insistent. She argued that every woman could be made beautiful when using the right tools.

At Karen's insistence, I first signed up for a self-improvement course. But then, as I began to have more confidence, I continued my lessons in modeling and soon became a full-fledged fashion model with a diploma from WTMA. They taught me to walk, talk, dress, apply makeup, and make the best of my looks and wardrobe. I learned that it was not necessary to have many changes of clothes in order to look elegant. One basic black dress was all one needed, as it served as foundation for a range of different looks. With the aid of proper accessories, perfect posture, and makeup, one can easily be transformed into an attractive person.

After learning how to make the best use of my assets, my attitude improved, as well. I often thought how my mother would certainly have approved of my efforts to become a lady. With my self-esteem in top form, I began the second major transition in my life. I had gone from childhood to motherhood, and now I was going to have a career.

WALTER THORNTON GRADUATION DAY

* * *

It had been nearly a year since the disappearance of my children, and I was still without news of their whereabouts. Reconciling myself to the possibility of never seeing them again, I felt I had no choice but to turn back to God for answers. I visited churches,

not synagogues, since my horrible synagogue experience in
Budapest left me phobic. Besides, I also feared being identified as
a Jew, never knowing when and if I would be exposed to prejudices. To me, churches were a safe haven and the images were
comforting. It was a place where I could sit and contemplate in
absolute peace and quiet. I spent a lot of my time praying to little
Saint Thérèsa, to my mother and father, to any saint who would
listen. I prayed to Jesus, telling him how much I felt his pain on
the cross. Always seeking a purpose for my existence, I promised
myself that if I should lose my children permanently, I would
either become a nun or a missionary in Africa.

But in spite of the bleak outlook, deep in my heart, I refused to
give up hope. I retained the attorney's services for some time,
begging him to continue his investigation. While searching for my
children, and mainly because of them, I kept true to my objective,
always trying to improve my life, my brain, and myself in general.
I no longer wanted to be just a waitress.

After graduation, Karen and I began our career as models. I
remember us parading along the streets with pride and elegance,
applying our professional walk intentionally, so we were easily
identifiable as models. We loved the looks of admiration we got
from both men and women as we passed and heard their whis-
pers: "They must be models." All the attention fooled us into
believing we were somehow superior. But even with our newly
acquired polish, modeling assignments were irregular and money
was scarce. By this time both Karen and I worked in offices
between our modeling jobs. Still, despite all of our diligent efforts,
most of the time we could hardly come up with our rent money,
so when an opportunity arose we would gladly accept dates from
admirers just for the sake of a free dinner. It seems callous in retrospect, but we called them our "meal tickets."

On one of these occasions, our meal tickets came highly recommended by some of Karen's office friends. They were two IBM employees who were in town on a computer- and language-training course from Quebec City. Karen and I took pains to dress ourselves fashionably, in the manner of our profession. We were yearning to be wined and dined at an elegant restaurant. As soon as the bell rang, Karen and I both ran down the stairs to answer the door, whereupon we found ourselves facing two tall, well-dressed men who politely removed their hats while they checked us out. Since our dates were not specifically assigned, it was clear from the start that both men gravitated toward Karen, but since Carl was the faster of the two to reach out, he won Karen while Andre was left without choice, me.

CHAPTER 15

Andre and Religion

━━━━━━━━━━━━━

As we had hoped, our dates took us to a lovely restaurant—since the bill was on IBM, anyway—and after dinner we went to an IBM party at someone's apartment. The place was packed with partygoers who cared much less about conversation than they did about drinking and loud music. Since I was never much of a party girl, I decided to venture elsewhere in the apartment for a little peace and relaxation, and that's when I heard classical music coming from one of the rooms. Tentatively I stepped inside. To my surprise I found my date, Andre, alone, stretched out on a bed—listening to Mendelssohn's Violin Concerto. I was very familiar with the music, for I had listened to it many times before both with Miss Maria at the orphanage, as well as at the rabbi's home. It was one of my favorites and I quietly sat down to listen. Andre looked at me, and, without exchanging a word, we communicated on a deeper level through the magical sound of the violin. When the piece was ended, Andre turned to me and kissed my hand.

Andre was born in Quebec City to an affluent, devoutly Catholic French-Canadian family. His father was a well-known doctor in Quebec City; his older brother was a doctor in Montreal, his sister a dietician, and his other brother an artist. Andre was just the sort of man I was hoping to find as a father figure for my children. He had class, he had education, he was refined. From that day forward, we saw a lot of each other. We took weekend trips in his little Volkswagen, went to concerts, listened to Bach, Mozart, and Beethoven. We shared books and poetry—both in French and English—and many more cultural pleasures that set the stage for us falling in love.

Four more years went by before I received a letter from my attorney informing me that my children had been located at last. They were under the protection of the Jewish Child Welfare Bureau, and living in Montreal. After Frank kidnapped them, he apparently returned with them to Montreal, where he filed a claim against me, accusing me of having abandoned them, of being a whore and an unfit mother, and then turned them over to the welfare bureau for protective custody. Elizabeth and Harry were placed into a foster home. Because of the sworn and signed affidavit Frank filed against me (which was full of lies), I had to undergo a series of psychological tests and a thorough investigation before I was finally given permission to write them and to visit them. And even though my letters were censored, I was grateful to have gained the right to correspond with them on a regular basis.

When word came that I had satisfied both the welfare bureau's investigation and the requirements of their compliance program, I was finally given the visiting rights for which I had waited so long. As I was still living in Toronto, Andre immediately offered to drive me back to Montreal. We said goodbye to Karen and headed to the city in which my children had been detained for over six years. I was puzzled why there had never been any real search conducted for their rightful mother.

To think that I was about to see my children after six long years made me beyond nervous and apprehensive. Although I was fully prepared to undergo any test, numerous questions and scenarios were fluctuating in my head. I wanted so much for them to love me, to make them happy, to make up for lost time. Being poorly fixed financially, I took out a loan from the Household Finance company and purchased a pretty dress for Elizabeth and a Mickey Mouse watch for Harry, which was what he had requested in one of his letters.

We arrived in Montreal in the early afternoon. Andre suggested we stop and relax at a nearby restaurant for a bite, and take a break after our long journey. No sooner did we sit down than everything went pitch black. The next time I opened my eyes I found myself staring at the stark white ceiling of the emergency room from a hospital bed. My extreme anxiety had caused me to pass out. I thanked God Andre was by my side to support me when I was released a couple of hours later.

Since my children had been so young when last I saw them, I wondered if they would even remember me. I knew that six years of separation at such a tender age must have had a terrible impact on them. What if they didn't recognize me? What if they didn't want me? What if…what if…what if…? Terrible fears and concerns suppressed any joy I might have otherwise felt in anticipation of our reunion.

In many ways, our projected reunion reminded me of the times I had reunited with my mother or father following a long absence. I could never forget the pain I felt each time I had to be separated from my parents. That pain could only be equaled by the joy I experienced upon seeing them again. I wondered if, I hoped that my children—who hardly knew me after all those years— would feel the same love for me as I had felt for my parents. I was frightened.

ANDRE WITH MY CHILDREN. OUR FIRST OUTING
AFTER THE KIDNAPPING.

By the time we reached my children's address it was late afternoon. Their apartment house was situated in a middle-class neighborhood. We climbed up two flights of stairs with Andre holding my arms as my knees were shaking and I felt weak. It was Andre who rang the doorbell. At last Mrs. Green, a short woman with grayish hair and sunken eyes, came to the door. She welcomed us with what struck me as a forced smile, then led us into the living room before she called out to the children. There was what seemed an endless awkward moment when my children arrived and we all stood around silently facing each other.

Although they had grown, their little faces still had the same expression I remembered. They looked a little pale and timid, but otherwise none the worse for wear. At the risk of coming on too forcefully and breaking into tears, I maintained some reasonable distance for a brief moment, but then finally I reached out to them, threw my arms around them, and held their delicious little bodies tightly in my arms for some time.

Mr. and Mrs. Green were a working-class, middle-aged couple with limited education. Mr. Green was a short, chubby, mousy cab driver. The couple had one child, a girl, who was married, and living away from home. Surviving on a cab driver's salary was a challenge to them, and it was no doubt what led Mrs. Green to become a foster parent. It was certainly not her love for children.

After our first reunion, I was given permission to visit my children every weekend. During those visits we played in the parks, shopped, went to the zoo and the amusement park; I tried to find something fun for them to do every weekend. During all the times my children and I spent together I was never told, nor did I have any inkling, that Mrs. Green was oftentimes abusive and beat them. That revelation was withheld from me until many years later when Harry and Elizabeth were grown up. From my perspective at the time, the children, however poor, lived in a fairly decent environment. They went to school and they had friends. The only thing they seemed to lack was better living quarters and the sort of manners I would have liked them to have. Still, there was nothing much I could do about these issues until I was awarded full custody of them.

Meanwhile, Andre's training period in Toronto came to an end, which meant he had to return to Quebec City where he ordinarily worked and lived with his parents. By then, I had totally moved back to Montreal, and rented a quaint little apartment not too far from my children. Before we said goodbye, Andre bought me a gift, a book called *The Little Prince*. "This is one of my favorite books," he said. "I want you to have it." Then we lay down next to each other on top of the bed, and he read out loud to me while I listened.

> "*Grown-ups love figures. When you tell them that you have made a new friend, they never ask you any questions about essential matters. They never say to you, 'What does his voice sound like? What games does he love best? Does he collect butterflies?' Instead, they*

demand: 'How old is he? How many brothers has he?
How much does he weigh? How much money does his
father make?' Only from these figures do they think
they have learned anything about him." —Antoine
de Saint-Exupéry

Andre put the book aside, took me in his arms, and embraced
me. He said that no matter what happened to us, he would never
forget me. We made the usual lovers' promises—we would keep
in close touch and stay in love forever. Our plan was for him to
settle in Quebec, introduce me to his parents, then as soon as I
gained full custody of the children I was to join him and we would
get married. Finally, he got off from the bed, took his hat, and
walked to the door. "I will call you as soon as I get home," he said.
I followed him to the door; we kissed each other goodbye and the
next minute he was gone.

Almost a week went by before I heard from him again. On the
telephone his voice sounded troubled and distant. He said he was
very sorry, but that due to his parents' wishes, he was being forced
to marry a French-Canadian woman. He said that his parents'
objections to me were manifold: I was not Catholic; I had been
previously married; I had two children; I was two years older than
Andre; I was a fashion model; and, finally, I was Hungarian. That
was the last I heard from Andre until many years later, when I
found that his wife could not bear children, that she was older
then he, and that she never ever loved him. Sadly, Andre died in
his early sixties a very unhappy man.

* * *

I mourned the loss of Andre and the pain lingered on. At the same
time, I was busy trying to survive. Because I could not find a job,

there were days when I went without food and sat in my little basement apartment crying my eyes out. I felt a terrible letdown. I felt very alone, without any hope on the horizon. Although I had access to my children, I could not find the means to support them. Often I was forced to ration what little food I had. If I bought a bowl of soup in the restaurant I had to save the bread that came with it for the following day to save myself from fainting of hunger. At times I was so hungry that I would have welcomed a bag of moldy bread.

In retrospect I am not sure why I could not get myself hired. Perhaps it was due to my modeling-type appearance. People did not think me capable of holding down an office job and I was even refused waitressing positions. It seemed that I was cursed for some reason. And, since nothing I tried worked to my advantage, in desperation I turned to God, asking for help. After my experience with Andre, I felt persecuted. I began to believe that it was religion that stopped me from moving forward. After all, I reasoned, I could have been married to Andre had I been born Catholic. Or maybe I couldn't get a job because I was a Jew? I suppose these doubts and anxieties were a natural consequence of my experiences during the war. No matter how I came by them, on these occasions I became angry with God. I could not comprehend how a God who was supposed to be all-merciful, a God who personified love, a God all-perfect and pure in every way would allow so much suffering, so much unhappiness, so many tragedies! Where was this God when the Germans killed my father, when the massacre occurred at the Danube? Who was this God who robbed me of my mother so early in my childhood? If God truly existed, how was it that he allowed so many murders, left so many orphans, and separated lovers? I was determined to find out and headed straight to the Catholic Information Center that was run by the Jesuits in downtown Montreal.

I was kindly received by a volunteer at the front desk whose name was Mrs. Norman. She gave me some brochures about the catechism, then introduced me to a British priest, Father Dickinson. Father Dickinson was of medium height and slim, with a long beard and a very pleasant demeanor. He was most welcoming, appeared very knowledgeable, and showed much personal interest in teaching me. When he was appointed as my mentor I went to him trustingly—eager to learn the answers to my questions and increase my limited knowledge about God.

Finding the journey to knowledge fascinating and satisfying, it wasn't long before my involvement with the center became my major focus. Mrs. Norman took a liking to me and became my surrogate mother. I studied; I volunteered; I tried hard to do all the good Christian kinds of things that were expected of me. After all, I was on the verge of finding answers to my questions, I was getting closer to understanding the nature of the Holy Spirit that in turn lifted my spirits to a higher level in life. That is, until the day when Father Dickinson suddenly transformed from being a priest to being an ordinary man, and started making physical advances. His unwelcome gestures came as a total shock, for I was of the belief that nuns and priests were the closest beings to sainthood, that they were above and beyond all mortal sins, that they were the messengers of God!

Shattered and betrayed, I told no one, not even the very kind Mrs. Norman. Instead I left the center forever. From then on I rejected any and all teachings of formal religion. It became my belief that if God is everywhere, I didn't have to attach myself to any religious organization. To my great relief, Mrs. Norman never questioned my change of heart, and we remained very close until the day she passed on.

While my questions about God remained unanswered, I did learn that giving is better than receiving; that the ability to forgive is an important aspect of achieving a peaceful, happy life; and that hatred is a self-imposed punishment. Thinking along these lines, I became increasingly confident with each visit with my children that someday we would become a family again. Now, instead of nursing my anger toward Frank and the welfare system, or detesting Mrs. Green who was not terribly cooperative during my visits, I tried looking at the bright side, believing that soon my children and I could begin a new life together.

On our first outings we were a bit distant with each other, and I was filled with much apprehension. But with each visit, our relationship grew a little deeper, fostering in me some hope for the future. Harry was more approachable than Elizabeth, who by nature was more reserved. She remained aloof and cautious, and was always very protective of her little brother. What I did not realize at the time, but discovered many years later, was that my children had been fed false information about me during our separation. They were brainwashed—made to believe that I had abandoned them. To this day, even as grownups I suspect that they still nurse that concept deep down inside, only now, they have elected to forgive me.

CHAPTER 16

In Pursuit of Happiness

IN THE ENSUING MONTHS, the welfare office gave me clearance to visit my children as often as I liked. However, I would not be eligible for full custody unless I demonstrated that I was a stay-at-home mother with a certain level of income. Since I had to work to earn a living, I could not foresee how as a single parent I could earn enough to support my two children and yet stay home. The concept seemed inconceivable especially since my profession was either modeling or waitressing. In desperate need for answers, I turned to God once more.

My prayers were answered when I finally got a break from the Constance Brown Modeling Agency. Miss Brown, the head of the agency, liked my work and signed me up, and supplied me with regular showroom and fashion show assignments. Gradually, my career as a fashion model began to take off. As my popularity as a model increased, I no longer had to think about finding work as a waitress. In spite of having lost my chance to marry the man I loved, I still had my children, my youth, and that eternal hope for the future. So often did I envision my children living with me under the same roof day in and day out—that we would be a family! Although at times I secretly doubted my ability as a parent—perhaps because of Frank's accusations, or maybe because I had never really experienced a true family life—I remained determined. After all, I had studied psychology and I was sure it would help me!

Now that I was nearing thirty, it seemed that I was finally headed in the right direction. Andre or no Andre, my life was moving forward. I had the luxury of being able to visit my children as often as I wanted which helped us getting bonded. My frequent modeling assignments allowed us to save a little money, and Frank had seemingly lost interest in us and stayed completely out of the picture. Aside from a couple of visits after he had first dropped the children off at the foster home, he never showed any further interest. He never visited or even telephoned the children.

My mission to improve myself remained a priority, especially now that I was able to be with Elizabeth and Harry again. I wanted to set a good example so that they could be proud of me. Since I could not afford a college education, I was determined to befriend the sort of people from whom I could learn. My love for jazz awakened a deep interest in art. To me jazz and the ability to express oneself with color, shape, and movement were related and intertwined. Soon I discovered that people who shared these interests were also spiritually uplifting and generally intellectual.

There was a jazz club in Montreal near the school of fine arts that attracted scholars, poets, writers, musicians, and painters. Those who were part of that scene were called the Montreal Bohemians.

We were the avant-garde—the beatniks. Pierre, my new and very distinguished boyfriend, was the director of the Canadian Broadcasting Corporation's art department. He was an artist and a scholar as well as a respected cyclist and mountain climber. He made me feel special. With Pierre's encouragement, I signed up as a student at the Montreal School of Fine Arts.

THE MONTREAL BOHEMIANS—PIERRE IS TO MY RIGHT

Although I was not a student of great ability, I did enjoy being amongst talented, ambitious artists and scholars. I loved mingling with them. I loved that they thought outside the box, that they were different from the everyday crowd, that they freely expressed their emotions and opinions.

It was in an art class that I met Louise, who was to become one of my best friends. We were the same age, and had the same passion for art. Although Louise was far more talented than I, we loved each other's work, and encouraged each other, talking for hours about colors, shapes, and forms. Louise was truly my inspiration.

My life became a continuous effort toward improvement. I loved my visits with my children. I loved my friends. I loved my work, and the money I was earning as a model allowed me to have daily meals, which for me was a novel concept.

Still, in order to get custody of my children, I needed much more. I needed *money*. Little did I know how greatly my life was going to change with a single phone call from the Constance Brown Agency.

"Can you come to the office for a tryout right away?" Miss Brown said.

Could I! I did not walk but rushed off in a taxi to the studio where I found more than a dozen models already waiting their turn for a chance at showcasing their craft.

"This will be a very special assignment, girls," Miss Brown told us. "If you're hired, you'll have at least six weeks' worth of steady work, all expenses paid. The salary is excellent. This is a good client of ours, so I want you to do your very best presentation. Understood?"

So there I was in line with a lot of other models who I thought were much prettier than me, waiting my turn to model for a man who had the power to make or break me.

Part of my collection

Girl with Flower

The Family

Forest in Winter

The Visitors

On the Beach

Guard

ACRYLIC PAINTINGS - PARTIAL COLLECTION

We all wore our basic black modeling dress as we walked into the room to take our turn. We posed; we walked; we turned; then left the room and waited to find out which one of us would be selected. We all knew the man only needed one model! After a long wait, Miss Brown came out and sent us home. She said she would get back to us within a couple of days.

Knowing this was a well-paying job, I prayed with all my heart to be the one selected. The salary was so high that I could put enough money aside to rent a house and get my children back. As I lay on top of my bed, daydreaming about a better future, the phone rang. I didn't let it ring more than once before I answered it. It was Miss Brown. By some miracle, I was the chosen one!

CHAPTER 17

Modeling

GASTON, MY NEW BOSS, had been born on a farm in Belgium. He went into the fashion business after he immigrated to Canada. When I met him, he was in his early thirties and married with three daughters. He was energetic and loved playing sports, especially soccer. He had blue eyes and blondish hair and loved to laugh and live in the moment.

I was twenty-eight when I accepted the assignment of traveling with him, modeling his line of suits, coats, hats, shoes, and gloves, all imported from France and Winnipeg. We left Montreal the day after I got the call, and from then on, we traveled across the province of Quebec from showroom to showroom. During our journey we soon discovered that we made a good team; our sales were very good. Customers loved us and it reflected significantly on Gaston's overall profits.

My keen desire to be *somebody* resurfaced when I was doing fashion shows. It was a startling but exhilarating sensation doing the model's catwalk on stage, to have people look up to me with so much envy and admiration. Imagine, me, a little nobody from Hungary who once walked around with newspaper wrapped around her feet, who had worn rags for clothing and a makeshift turban to cover her bald head—I was now the envy of men and women! How I wished my grandmother or any of my family could have seen me. There were times when after the fashion show I would be asked for my autograph! *Me* giving autographs! I think my parents would have been proud.

Since Gaston was a father himself, he could fully comprehend the pain I had suffered through the loss of my children, and he understood my desire to get them back. During our long journeys between cities, we had plenty of opportunity to either plan our next sale strategy, or to discuss the possibility of how and when I would gain custody of my little family. Eager to help me, Gaston spent a lot of time talking with me about my future, which I found very flattering. No one that I knew cared more about me. My friend Karen had blended into oblivion once I moved back to Montreal, Louise was busy with her family, and Pierre was lacking the compassion I needed for understanding family affairs. So when Gaston and I exchanged intimate details of our personal lives, past and present, it made me feel important. I was happy thinking that I was helping him also, by being such a good friend.

This was when I learned about Gaston's unhappy marriage. He candidly admitted that he had chosen a profession in which there was much traveling in order to distance himself from his nasty, nagging wife.

MODELING FOR CONSTANCE BROWN AGENCY

MODELING FOR GASTON'S COMPANY

Our workload was very intense. It required carrying merchandise such as heavy coats and suits in and out of hotels; setting up the rooms; repeatedly describing the quality of the goods; and dealing with a variety of personalities. The buyers in particular were very often demanding and abrasive. By evening, both Gaston and I were exhausted, and after dinner we would retire to our respective rooms until we'd meet again the next morning.

Then one night, after a hard day of work, our routine changed. Instead of a quick meal, Gaston invited me out to a special celebration since we had made one of our most successful sales yet. A large department store chain, a new client, had placed a huge order. Gaston was in very high spirits. He took me to an expensive restaurant with white tablecloths, candlelight, wine, and music. We had a lovely dinner; we talked, laughed, danced, and even discussed some of our selling strategies late into the evening. After dinner, we said good night, and I settled in for the night as usual in my room. I was just about to slip into my nightgown when there was a knock on my door. I heard Gaston softly calling my name, asking, "Are you still up?" There was an urgency in his voice.

"Yes, I'm still up," I answered him through the door. "Are you all right?"

"No," he said. "I have a terrible headache. Do you have any aspirin?"

I quickly put on a robe and unlocked the door to let him in.

Gaston walked past me without a glance, went straight to the window overlooking the courtyard, then nervously lit a cigarette. He offered me one. His hands were shaking as he lit the match. I began to think that something terrible might have happened to his family. "Is it the children?" I asked, concerned.

He inhaled the smoke deeply into his lungs, and paused. Then, with tears in his eyes, he said, "No, it's not the children, it's you. I want you to know that I have never loved anyone in my life as much as I love you. Please tell me it's okay. How do you feel about me? Do you love me too?"

Gaston's confession did not entirely surprise me. I had suspected for some time that he loved me. I had come to love him too. We fell into each other's embrace, sharing the unrestricted warmth of our bodies.

I had never known this level of desire till Gaston. Certainly Frank had not cared for me in that way, and Andre had not been a terribly physical person. So I was intoxicated by the sensation of Gaston's heightened breathing while he whispered his feelings of passion and desire. Selfishly disregarding his wife, his children, my children, I welcomed his kisses and reciprocated with equal fervor. We consummated our love and satisfied our hunger for each other for days thereafter, allowing ourselves the pleasures of our forbidden but mutual love.

Although Gaston lacked the finesse and education I wanted in a father figure for my children, his love, his passion, and our romantic interludes distracted me from my original plan. I loved that Gaston hungered for me. And I loved that he was very protective. This part of our relationship offered a kind of substitute father's affection. I loved that he made me feel safe and paid attention to my needs. For the first time in my life I was truly in love and deliriously happy.

At last, I had found someone who genuinely cared for me. In time our passion grew even deeper, and while under the spell of romance, Gaston promised me the sun, the moon, and the stars—but most important of all, he promised to help me get my children back.

Of course there was the matter of Gaston's marriage and his own children, an issue that stood between us like a dormant volcano just waiting to erupt. But because we were swept away—our love was too wonderful to spoil with unpleasant matters—we elected to ignore such things while we were wrapped in each other's arms. It wasn't until he got out of my bed to go home to his wife that I became tormented by the vision of him with another woman. When I told him of my feelings, Gaston responded by promising me a home, my children, and the eventual separation from his wife. He assured me that he had a plan, and with that I had to be content.

Gaston did have a plan and he did keep his promise. First, he rented us a charming two-story house on an island just outside of Montreal. It had a garden in front and back, and the rapids rushed past our backyard. A bonus for me was that my dear friends Louise and her husband Hubert lived only two houses down the road from us. This made our move even more appealing. Once we had secured our housing, we went to the Child Welfare Service to post proof of my fixed income. Gaston signed papers confirming that, as my boss, he would guarantee me work from home and that my salary would be commensurate with my needs. Having met the welfare bureau's criteria, I finally obtained full legal custody of my children after six years of struggle. I had never known greater joy!

CHAPTER 18

Our New Family

~~~~~~~~~~~~~~~~

OUR HOUSE ON THE ISLAND was something out of a dream. We were surrounded by respectable private homes. Trees and flowers were everywhere. We had a private dock where we could park a canoe or a boat. The garden in the back had steps that led directly to the river and our private beach. The house itself was spacious, with a fireplace in the living room. The children were admitted to a high school nearby, and soon our house became the gathering place for all their friends. In addition, Gaston gave us a German shepherd, Sultan, who became our devoted guardian. Harry took up guitar, and Elizabeth acquired a boyfriend who was the son of the island's very own police officer, a prestigious position.

Gaston bought a lovely, bright yellow motorboat, which he anchored alongside our house. He would take Harry out water-skiing or fishing, and sometimes he even let Harry navigate the boat alone. Our lives were falling into place. We were a happy family—until the next incident.

A FAMILY AT LAST!

Since the island's public beach was practically in our backyard, our neighbors who lived there would often spend time boating, swimming, and picnicking. Louise and I frequently took our children there. We enjoyed watching our children play in the water while the two of us sat and chatted. On one of these happy occasions I suddenly felt a strange presence behind me. It was the same terrible feeling I once felt in the Toronto restaurant. I turned to see what it was, and I saw Frank standing there looking down at me with a sly grin on his face.

For a brief moment I thought I was having a bad dream. How could he have found me? How did he know?

Louise took one look at me and asked, "What's the matter? Are you okay?"

I felt so faint that I could hardly answer. But I told Louise to go call Gaston and the police. Then, realizing that showing fear would only encourage Frank to further intimidate me, I summoned up my strength, stood up to face him, and asked him what he wanted as if I didn't know.

"I want to see my children," he bluntly demanded. Even though Elizabeth and Harry were not too far away, he didn't even recognize them since he had not seen them in years!

"Of course," I replied. "You want to see them? Come—I will take you to them." Outwardly I was calm and collected, but inside I was trembling like a jellyfish. I quickly gathered up my things and left the beach, with Frank trailing behind me.

As we headed down the road, I was reminded of the time in Hungary, when those men were about to turn me over to the police. I figured that if I was able to fake my bravery then, certainly I should have no trouble dealing with Frank now. But what was it that Frank really wanted? What was his purpose, I wondered. It had been years since he last saw Harry and Elizabeth. He could not even recognize them! Apparently he had neglected to consider that by now the children were teenagers. And this time I had legal custody of them. Remembering my legal rights, I was much less apprehensive than I had been at first, although there was still his tendency toward violence that needed to be considered.

I led Frank to the house of a policeman that I knew, thankful that Frank must have thought we were going to my place. I rang the bell and the officer came to the door, already aware of the situation thanks to Louise. The officer questioned Frank about his right to visit, then instructed Frank not to return to the island again until he was able to procure legal papers for his visiting rights.

Even though Frank was gone, I was left feeling very insecure. Gaston assured me that I had nothing to worry about, that he and Sultan, our German shepherd, would take care of Frank if and when he was to return. In preparation for such an event, Gaston proceeded to train Sultan to attack on command. The trouble was, Gaston had no experience in dog training so when he wrapped a heavy padding around his arm and shouted "Attack!" the dog obediently went straight for Gaston's arm. So from then on, every time Sultan heard the command "Attack," he always went immediately to Gaston's arm. Realizing his training was futile Gaston needed to find a new solution for our protection. As a last resort he completely changed his tactics, and summoned Harry and Elizabeth in preparation for the next episode. He asked them straight out, "How do you feel about Frank? Do you wish to see him again, or not? If the answer is no, you will need to tell him so yourself."

The children hardly knew Frank; they seemed very nonchalant about the situation and expressed no particular desire to see or be with their father again.

It was Christmastime when the next incident with Frank occurred. Gaston and I were in the living room, busy putting up the Christmas tree, when Sultan started barking even before the doorbell rang. The children were upstairs in their rooms studying, so it was Gaston who went to answer the door. This time Frank came with false documents, claiming his right to take the children. Gaston easily recognized Frank's scam, and since Gaston was always game for a confrontation, he invited Frank into the living room. "Take a seat," Gaston said, then he commanded our formidable canine to sit and guard our unwanted guest. Frank sat motionless, visibly terrified of Sultan when Gaston left him alone in the room.

Gaston summoned Elizabeth and Harry into the kitchen for a brief conference. He told them that the time had come for them to face Frank once and for all with their decision. For the last time, did they or did they not want to see their father again? He told them they needed to give their answer to Frank directly. Although it had to be difficult for my children to reject their own flesh and blood, they chose to confront him, and they bravely turned Frank down for the last time. While it was a victory for me, I knew that it had to be heartbreaking for my children, so this was no time for me to rejoice.

CHAPTER 19

The Wicked Stepsisters

Now that he was happy at home Gaston was unwilling to travel, so he exchanged his fashion business for a sporting goods store. Since Gaston was an excellent salesman, it wasn't long before his business became quite profitable, and soon he opened a second store and even a shop to build his own line of camping trailers. But no sooner had we settled our problem with Frank, thinking that finally our lives would be much safer, another problem emerged—this time, from Gaston's side of the family.

To start with, Gaston's wife Claudette categorically refused to give Gaston a divorce. All she wanted was to be compensated for her loss, not just monetarily, but in every way possible. She was on a mission of destruction, and used her children for ammunition.

There must have been signs of danger from the start, but I was naive enough to believe in the adage that love conquers all, and I would not be distracted by an opposing view. What I did not comprehend, and didn't know how to fight off, was evil. Gaston's family was seeking revenge! The conflict was not about Claudette wanting Gaston back, because she did not love him. It was about not wanting anyone else to have him. Thus, a war was declared between our families, with Claudette sending her troops—her two teenage girls—to battle. Since the third daughter was much younger than the two sisters, the little one was kept out of the family feud.

From the moment the girls, Monique and Celine, moved in with us, they made their mission clear. Operating on the information they were given by their mother, they thought of me as the whore who broke up their happy home life by stealing away their father. Naturally, the girls reacted accordingly, and almost immediately transformed our peaceful setting into a living nightmare. Although Gaston regarded his daughters' presence as an absolute victory over his wife, as far as my side of the family was concerned, our lives soon became unbearable. The two girls were always setting up traps. Often we realized that money was missing out of our wallets, or clothes disappeared and were never found, or Monique would claim she was being maltreated by one of us. One of the most offensive behaviors was when Celine would sneak into Harry's bed at night and make advances. To my shock, Gaston, in a state of utter denial, would blame Harry, and then a fight would start.

As the pressures and demands from Gaston's "first" family kept increasing, he soon found it difficult to cope, both financially and emotionally. In time, his fiscal obligations became progressively heavier, and since he was unable to promptly pay his suppliers, Gaston soon found himself dealing with many frustrated, angry vendors. To stay afloat, he ended up shifting payments from one to another, until he could no longer escape his creditors.

On top of all this, sixteen-year-old Monique got mixed up with a bad crowd and had to be bailed out of jail, only to find that she was pregnant. Although few words were spoken about the girl's unfortunate condition, there was an underlying current among her and her sister that held me responsible for the family's upheaval. *If she hadn't stolen our father* became their everlasting mantra.

At last Gaston concluded that since he was born and raised on a farm he should return to his natural roots, that city life was not for him. Suddenly he became convinced that country living would be better and healthier for all of us, especially the children. *Menez la vie simple!* With great decision he put his business up for sale, and began his intensive research for just the right farmland. The more he thought about it, the more excited he became. It wasn't long before he found what he was looking for: a two-story house, a large barn, a stable, all on 200 acres of mountainous land in Eastern Townships, about a two-hour drive from Montreal, and not more than a half-mile from Vermont's American border.

CHAPTER 20

The Farm

NONE OF THE REST OF US WERE particularly ecstatic about becoming farmers. The closest I had ever gotten to horse manure was sitting on a horse-drawn carriage. Nevertheless, the prospect of possibly finding peace and happiness by living a simpler life away from the pressures of the city seemed plausible to me. Influenced by Gaston's way of thinking, I began to believe that a country lifestyle was healthy and down-to-earth, and surely it would help bring our two families closer together.

Our hearts full of hope, we moved into our new house. It had many rooms, but no central heating. There was but one furnace in the basement that had to be manually fed with wood and replenished in the middle of the night if we did not want to freeze to death during the harsh Canadian winters. Our days were long, since we had many chores. We got up with the sun to feed the animals, and there was always enough work to last us way into the evening.

Never a day went by without my looking longingly at the American mountains of Vermont only a short distance away. There it was, America practically at my back door, yet it was out of my reach. I had long ago become a Canadian citizen, yet I still had not fallen out of love with the notion of someday living in America. The land of endless opportunities!

Gaston's vision as a farmer was very ambitious. Aside from raising beef cattle, which he said would be our main source of income, he decided to also raise chickens and rabbits, which he surmised were profitable products due to their reproductive nature. Then, in the winter, he also planned to make our own maple syrup. He assured me that taking care of beef cattle was not going to be much of a chore since there would be no milking involved. All we needed to do was fill the feeder with food and shovel the manure, *et voilà!*

The house came with two cats that the sellers left behind, and these two cats rapidly multiplied into dozens. In no time at all we had nearly thirty cats. Unlike Gaston and his two girls, Elizabeth, Harry, and I adored every one of those furry creatures, each with its own personalities. We gave them names and they all knew who they were. Gaston would not let any of them in the house, and in fact, he was not even in favor of letting us feed them. In his view there were plenty of rats and mice running around to keep them alive.

We also had two horses that lived in a small stable located across the barn. We had a shed for chickens and another for breeding rabbits. Who knew that we would have the only impotent rabbits in the world? Instead of multiplying, they turned into carnivores. Elizabeth, who was in charge of the rabbits, was mortified when she discovered their half-eaten bodies in their cages. Who knew that rabbits could be cannibals? And if that were not enough, our chickens were all eaten or stolen by weasels and foxes that came down from the mountains at night.

Harry, Elizabeth, and I were given specific assignments on the farm. However, Gaston's two daughters were excluded from the program since Monique was pregnant and Celine claimed to have a bad back. In fact Celine acted almost like an invalid until it came time to do things she liked, such as driving the Ski-Doo, the tractor, or the car. By contrast, Harry was given many jobs. Along with whatever else had to be done on any given day, he was to attend to the cows and the horses, cut wood, shovel snow, and shovel manure. Gaston's excuse for taking advantage of my eighteen-year-old like this was that he needed to be molded into "a man"!

Aside from assisting in the barn, my job was to take care of all household chores, including the cooking, baking, laundry, and cleaning. Gaston would not eat store-made bread, pastries, or even mayonnaise. Everything had to be homemade. Once he even hired a French butcher from Montreal who came to our farm to kill one of our cows and then cut the meat the way Gaston liked it, packaging it to be piled into our freezers for future consumption.

The slaughtering experience left me absolutely horrified. Knowing the butcher was coming, I could not sleep the night before, and was kept awake many nights after that, still mourning the killing of that poor unsuspecting cow who had been led to slaughter. The blood, the cry of the animal! It took me back to the Danube! How were we different from the Nazis or the Arrow Cross? I was both heartbroken and nauseous. The day of the slaughter I could not go outside the house. Instead, I sat by the window in the bedroom and gazed yearningly at the amazing American mountains in Vermont.

There were some things about farming that I absolutely hated. Gaston forced me to go to the livestock auctions, where animals were herded into stalls, often beaten and shoved around without consideration. These instances never failed to trigger flashbacks to the war. They were a constant reminder that I had witnessed innocent people being treated the same way. I started resenting Gaston for forcing me to relive my nightmares.

During the course of my work in the barn I had developed a special relationship with our cows. I gave them names according their personalities. Contrary to what some people think, cows do have personalities. When Isabelle, one of our Holstein cows, gave birth to her calf, I named it Bambi. Isabelle was such a caring, loving mother that at times she put my motherhood to shame. Not only was she caring for her own offspring, but she was often open to adopting orphaned calves and treated them as her own. Not all cows are willing to do that. Then there was Maria, a dark brown cow with horns and a feisty Latin kind of personality. Maria did not take any nonsense from anyone. At feeding time, she always had to be the first. Then there was gentle Sally, whose light beige coat and calm manner reminded me of that British "stiff upper lip" elegance. Collectively these cows gave me a better insight into the animal world. They taught me that they had feelings, and they were indeed dedicated mothers to their calves. I loved them all. Then to see them shoved and pushed around at auctions and finally taken to slaughter was simply more than my heart was able to handle. I cried a lot in those days. Gaston thought that I was completely out of my mind.

THE THREE OF US ON THE FARM WITH ONE OF OUR 27 CATS

MY GOOD FRIEND ISABELLE

He could not comprehend how I could possibly compare animals to people. With pressures coming from all sides, Gaston and I had many conflicts to overcome. We fought about many things, but mostly we fought over our children. However, there were occasions when we would let our guards down. Sometimes Gaston would take me on a long hike across our property. There were pine and maple trees, a lovely little river in the higher wooded areas, and deer and wild rabbits would graze along our path. At times like these, Gaston would become very romantic, and it was comforting to know that we were treading on our very own land. We had so much, that even if we were to run around stark naked, no one could have seen us since it was our very own private territory all fenced in!

On more than one occasion, Gaston and I took advantage of our freedom while in the forest and rekindled the passion we once knew at the beginning of our relationship. It was after one of these times that Gaston surprised me with a gift—a beautiful brown coat that he knew I always wanted. His unusually kind gesture took me completely by surprise. For a brief moment, I was happy, not just because of the gift, but that Gaston thought enough about me to give me something I had longed for. For a brief moment I was foolish enough to believe that perhaps things for us could change. But my hope was soon crushed when Monique saw the coat. Her face distorted with jealousy, she made such a fuss that Gaston took the coat from me and gave it to her, promising me that one day he would replace it.

All this time, Gaston had no qualms about having his daughters living with us. It was really what he wanted, for they were his pride and joy, but most importantly he relished the idea of triumphing over his wife. Gaston truly believed that his daughters loved him, when in actual reality, the two girls loved no one.

They were simply two miserable, self-centered souls.

As the months passed, my children and I became full-fledged farmers, and worked long and hard for our keep. Gaston, for his part, took over one of the rooms downstairs to set up his own office. From then on, he spent most of his time sitting there alone, smoking and staring into space for long periods of time. When I questioned him about his seclusion, he said he was contemplating our survival strategy.

Sadly, his contemplation did not bear much fruit. As his money ran out and nothing was coming in, he started applying his old Ponzi scheme, robbing one creditor to pay the other. Each time the phone rang he instructed me to answer, and say: "Sorry. He's not home. Can I take a message?"

The winters in Canada can be pretty harsh. Money or not, the cattle and the family had to be fed, and the house had to be heated. Since we were desperately short of funds, Gaston decided to transform our home into a bed-and-breakfast place for skiers. So it was that before long I became the "innkeeper." I was the baker, the chambermaid, the cook, the cleaning woman, the hostess, and farmer all rolled into one. In one year I had transitioned from a reputable fashion model into a common farmer and a slaving housewife.

Being so close to ski resorts such as Sutton on the Canadian side and Vermont on the American, we had no problem filling our rooms. While I worked very hard to please our guests, my only reward was getting to know some lovely, normal people with whom I could have a reasonably intelligent conversation, a luxury of which I was deprived with Gaston. Over the months I had begun to notice that Gaston's mental health had steadily declined.

He began to show some serious signs of peculiarities.

It became quite noticeable that his mood swings at times transformed him from a kindly Dr. Jekyll to a monstrous Mr. Hyde; this was of course very troubling. I became increasingly apprehensive in his presence, not knowing which personality I would be dealing with at any given time. As our arguments became more frequent and intense, mostly over money or our children, there soon came a time when I was even unable to stand his presence. The passionate love I once felt for him was transformed into passionate hatred. Every gesture, every move Gaston made revolted me. Naturally, my feelings were reflected in our sex life, and when his advances toward me were rejected, he would go into a jealous rage, accusing me of having a fixation on Harry, my own son!

It was during haying season that I became acutely aware of Gaston's deteriorating mental state. The first recollection I have of his odd conduct happened on the first haying day. Upon the insistence of his robust but indolent sixteen-year-old tomboy daughter, Celine, Gaston appointed her to drive the tractor while Harry and I were made to follow the wagon, picking up sixty-pound bales of hay and throwing them onto the wagon. Up and down the hill under the scorching sun Harry and I labored all day like slaves while Gaston and his daughter drove the tractor exerting much less effort. But the incident that brought matters to a boil was that Celine made several obvious efforts to try and run me down with the tractor and then make it look like an accident. I knew that Gaston witnessed some of these incidents, and yet he never once intervened. In fact, later, when I mentioned it to him, it was I who was reprimanded for making a false accusation.

The second important sign of Gaston's instability occurred one day when one of our neighbors inadvertently trespassed on our land. Without warning, Gaston grabbed his rifle, ran out to the field, and fired at the unsuspecting man, nearly taking his life! Word about this incident traveled fast around our small village and, until I went around apologizing to all our neighbors, we were shunned by the entire community.

The final confirmation of Gaston's deteriorating mental state came not long after the shooting incident. It happened late one afternoon, following our hard day's work of lifting bales and piling them high into the barn. All of us who had worked collapsed in the living room to watch *Bonanza* on television. All of us except Gaston who retired to his office—or so we thought. Suddenly I heard some crackling sounds coming from outside and from the corner of my eye I could see lights flickering not too far away. "What is that?" I asked out loud, and when I turned around the answer lay right in front of me. I saw huge flames shooting into the sky from the barn. Horrified, I called out for Gaston and ran to his office, but he wasn't there. I searched for him frantically, but could not find him anywhere. Panicked, I called the fire department.

Since the barn was full of hay, the flames caught quickly. Before the fire trucks could reach us, the fire had already spread rapidly; flames shot high into the sky. Before long the barn, all the hay, and everything in the surrounding area was completely engulfed including the fences and the grass out on the field. Soon the flames reached the stable across the yard and it wasn't long before they would reach our house as well. Fearing that our cows and cats had to be inside burning alive I screamed out Gaston's name repeatedly, but still, he did not respond. For a fraction of a second I feared that he might have been inside the barn with the animals. Feeling faint, I forced myself on weak legs to search around the stable when all at once I spotted Gaston behind the smoke, way out into the field chasing the cows and the horses as far into the mountains as possible. Although for a moment I wondered how Gaston could have gotten that far in so little time, I was much too concerned about saving our house, our cars, and our cats to give it a second thought.

The old wooden barn incinerated rapidly as the flames danced from fence to fence, spreading far into the distance. Later I learned that the effects of the heat were sufficiently intense to be felt across the American border. The fire trucks that came were soon followed by many of our concerned neighbors, all trying to give us a hand. Setting aside the shooting incident, everyone did their neighborly best to try and save our house, which after hours of hard labor luckily was a success.

That night as I lay in bed unable to fall asleep, I kept replaying the fire incident in my head. The more I thought about it the more I realized that it had to have been Gaston who started it all. Over the days that followed, my suspicions were confirmed when I overheard him talking to the insurance inspectors about rebuilding the barn. The fire was still smoldering outside, when Gaston had already drawn out a homemade blueprint of exactly what he wanted the new barn to look like and where he wanted it built. During the subsequent investigation I was never questioned by the insurance company, so I kept my silence, for fear of retaliation from Gaston.

As for me, seeing the smoldering fire and the ruins of the barn was a painful reminder of all the destruction I had witnessed in Budapest. I hated Gaston for causing so much harm to so many, and for once again taking me back into that nightmarish past I tried so hard to forget.

Even with the insurance money, we were short of funds, since Gaston was late with his mortgage payments and was in debt to most of his suppliers. It was at this time that he decided to send Harry off to work in nearby Sutton for a construction company. He was of the opinion that since Harry, still only eighteen, was not macho enough, hard labor would surely form him into a man. Although the work indeed proved to be hard, and the hours were long and the wages small, it suited Harry very well, for it gave him a chance to be out from under Gaston's condescending domination at least during working hours. Still, when Harry came home at night, even after his hard day's labor, Gaston would find some extra chores for him to do.

OUR HOUSE ON THE FARM IN
EASTERN TOWNSHIPS

Since we desperately needed every penny to make ends meet, I started baking and selling my homemade cookies as well as my artwork at the village's open-air market. I even had some of my paintings hanging outside of our house as advertisement.

It wasn't long before the new building materials for the barn started to arrive: metal, wood, nails, paint, and plaster. Our forgiving neighbors came in bunches to volunteer their time. In less than a month the cows had their shelter back, only this time the barn was built specifically for beef instead of dairy cattle; the cows were not restricted to stalls, since there would be no milking involved. While everyone was busy hammering and building, Gaston stood by and supervised with the blueprint and a cigarette in hand, but never took part in any hard labor.

* * *

No sooner was the fire put out and dealt with, when another disaster occurred. This incident was the biggest tragedy of all, for it involved breaking my son's heart. Somehow, and for some unknown reason, suddenly all of our cats came down with distemper. Unwilling to medicate, Gaston took matters into his own hand. He gathered all the cats into the basement underneath the house, then handed Harry a shotgun, and ordered him to shoot the helpless creatures execution-style, one by one. With trembling hands Harry obeyed.

"This will make a man out of you," Gaston snapped at nineteen-year-old Harry, who stood in a state of shock, for with his gentle nature he would have saved a fly from drowning.

I could not sleep that night. The next morning, Harry came to me and announced that he was leaving the farm. Although his news hurt me terribly, I completely approved of his decision. Neither the farm nor Gaston was a good match for him. The very next day Harry left without saying goodbye to Gaston. I was heartbroken as I watched him go, but I knew that if he wanted to remain his own person, he had no choice. His absence left me with a deep feeling of emptiness. I was guilt-ridden by the realization that I had let my son down once again. Frank must have been right. I was an unfit mother.

With life on the farm on a rapid decline, Elizabeth soon left as well. Her return to Montreal was the best thing for her, for she was quickly able to establish herself with a job working for an airline as well as finding an apartment where she felt peaceful and happy. And by the time Elizabeth was settled, Harry had packed his few belongings and left with a friend to go traveling in Europe.

In the wake of my children's exodus, Gaston's two daughters victoriously returned to their mother, and finally Gaston and I were left alone to our misery. I spent a great deal of time blaming myself for my repeated mistakes. What was it about me that made me choose all the wrong partners? First it was Frank, then Andre, then Gaston. Each time I tried to create a healthy family structure, I failed. Was it that I lacked a role model? What did it take to comprise a family if it wasn't one's dedication and the offer of love? I fell into a deep depression and concluded once again that my life was not worth living. Then, the more I thought about it, the more I began to realize that Gaston had played a major part in the disaster that had become our lives. I began to see that I had truly done my best; it was Gaston who had destroyed everything we tried to build up. The realization of this made me furious. I was unwilling to forgive Gaston for all the harm he had done—to all of us but especially to Harry.

Feeling helpless and vulnerable, I not only lost my will to live, but then, strangely, also my fear of Gaston. Since I had nothing more left to lose, I was no longer willing to compromise. I decided that the next time Gaston made any sort of derogatory remark about my children, particularly Harry, I was ready to counterattack.

Meanwhile, I took steps to leave the farm by secretly packing my belongings into plastic garbage bags bit by bit. My departure had to be carefully orchestrated since Gaston's personality had greatly changed, and we all knew he was capable of sudden violence. Also, I needed to save in order to move on, and since I was not given any pocket money, I had to pinch from our grocery expenses a little at a time. A friend who lived in the village knew of my miserable life with Gaston and since she wasn't fond of him either, she was willing to help me out and spared me some space in her garage where I could start hiding my belongings. Every time I drove to the village for food, I took another bag and a little bit of cash.

Now every day was a new day, filled with hope and the anticipation of freedom. I could hardly wait for the opportunity when I would confront Gaston with my news that I was leaving him once and for all. Finally, after several long, lonely weeks, the moment presented itself.

It happened one morning after breakfast. Gaston put on his jacket and was about to go to the new barn, about a half a mile across the pasture, to feed the animals. He turned to me and made a snide remark about Harry, then walked out, slamming the screen door. My blood boiled. I didn't say anything; instead I silently slipped on my coat, picked up the biggest knife I could find in the kitchen drawer, concealed it in my pocket, and followed him all the way down the road. Gaston was unaware that I was behind him, so when we reached the barn almost at the same time, I took him by surprise.

"What are you doing here?" he asked abruptly. Although I'm sure he could tell from the expression on my face that I wasn't paying a social call, he turned and went into the barn, purposely demonstrating that my presence didn't mean much to him. I followed him inside. He had picked up a pail of grain to feed the animals when I marched up to him and stopped him in his tracks. Fearlessly I looked straight into his eyes and said, "This is it! I've had enough!"

"What is your problem?" he asked coolly.

"You!" I said sharply. "You are my problem, you bastard! I'm sick and tired of your condescending attitude toward my son, toward all of us! You are a sick man!"

Gaston dropped his pail and came toward me, but I would not back up. Then I blurted out some more of my disdain for his constant bad-mouthing and the disparaging remarks about my children. Naturally Gaston retaliated in kind, and it wasn't long before our verbal exchange heated to a boil. Like two frustrated, enraged animals, we both shouted malicious accusations and brought up sensitive issues that were hurtful to us both. And then I accused him of arson.

This *really* set him off. All at once he was murderous! He charged toward me like a bull in a ring, but when he saw that I remained unintimidated he stopped in his tracks. Instead of backing off, I grabbed his jacket by the lapels and with herculean strength, I shoved him against the wall and pinned him in place. "You *bastard!"* I shouted. "If you think you're so macho, let me see you use this knife on me!" I pulled out the knife from my pocket and handed it to him. "Go ahead!" I screamed. "Be a man, show me you have the balls! Kill me! I'd much rather die than live with you for another day!"

My outrage actually calmed both of us down. It felt good to defend myself and to express all my frustrations at long last. Then, as I looked at Gaston's pale face, I saw nothing more than a weak, helpless, pitiful person whose macho exterior suddenly revealed a cowardly, frightened, miserable little man.

* * *

After the storm comes the calm. The following day, Gaston came to me like a lamb, promising me the moon, the sun, and the stars. He said he would give me anything I wanted if I'd be willing to reconcile. I told him all I wanted was my freedom, the very thing he refused to give me. So, on the surface at least, we compromised. He agreed to go for therapy on a weekly basis. He promised to take me across the border to America for a short vacation. He was going to change, he assured me, he was willing to go to any length to make our relationship work again. He swore that he would look after the few cows we had left and be responsible for all the other farm duties while I went to work as a receptionist in a nearby hospital to supplement our income.

At this I was left very confused. On the one hand, I wanted to believe that Gaston could or would change, and that we could live happily ever after, for I felt that I had nothing and no one else. On the other hand, I was skeptical of Gaston's promises, for how could a man turn his character around so radically? Was it possible that therapy could help that much? In the end I remained vigilant and kept alive my plan to escape. Each time Gaston left the house for therapy I packed more of my things and moved the bags into my friend's garage.

Gaston requested that I join him at one of his therapy sessions. He told me that the therapist needed to see us together in order to evaluate both sides of the story. Thinking this would be truly helpful for both of us, I consented.

As we sat in the therapist's office reviewing our "marital problems," it soon became clear that during all the visits Gaston had with the therapist prior to my arrival he had painted a picture of me consisting of nothing but lies. I was in shock to discover that he considered himself the victim—and that I was viewed as the perpetrator, the cause of everyone's unhappiness. By the time I arrived, the therapist had already concluded that I should be committed to an asylum!

As a result of this dreadful session, I began to experience anxiety attacks and became severely claustrophobic. I felt closed in everywhere I went, even at our familiar supermarket, and kept passing out. At first, I thought there was something physically wrong with me, but when I visited a doctor, he said, "Claustrophobia is a mental state, not a physical one." Still, I got to the point where I was afraid to leave the house. The only place I felt safe was at my job in the hospital. There at least doctors and nurses surrounded me, in case I should lose consciousness again. Finally I suffered a severe gallbladder attack, which then turned into a blessing in disguise.

* * *

Following surgery and during convalescence at the hospital I had time to reflect on my life. I thought about my dreams, my promises, my trials, my errors, and my experiences. I realized that I was a poor judge of character when it came to choosing the men in my life and that it was time for me to do some soul-searching. Just who exactly was I? What was my purpose in life? What was I doing wrong, and what could I do differently to prevent myself from making the same mistakes over and over again? I realized that once I recuperated from my illness, I would have an opportunity to start my life over again. This time it was imperative that I make some major changes.

The more I questioned who I was, the more I came to realize that I was seriously suffering from a lack of self-esteem. I once read that self-respect is the cornerstone of all virtue. But how can one earn self-respect without feeling the love of others? For as long as I could remember, I had always had a strong desire to be loved and accepted, but with the destruction of our family, I was left without much of that. I was either criticized or persecuted, making me believe that I was less deserving than others. Therefore, my need to be loved and to belong was so powerful that I allowed myself to be sidetracked, to make choices that were wrong for me. Even abuse was better than no attention at all. Yet I was also driven by my constant desire to better myself—if not for my own sake, for that of my children, my parents. Or to simply prove that I could.

When I left Hungary, I had promised myself I would go to America, but I never did. I had sworn that I would fulfill my mother's dying wishes and make something of myself, but I had not. Here I was past thirty years old with nothing to show for my years but two children who had gone out of my life once again. It seemed to me that my life consisted of a series of huge mistakes, and for that I hated myself.

While the surgery was a success, my mental state was gradually deteriorating. I became very depressed and emotionally nonresponsive. I developed a bladder infection and suffered from anxiety attacks. The doctors and the nurses, who knew me well, treated me as family. Most importantly, they shielded me from Gaston, and helped me hire an attorney who filed a restraining order against him. I was offered legal service without having to pay a retainer, since upon the discovery of Gaston's assets, it was revealed that he had accumulated many debts under my name by forging my signature. So my attorney was able to absolve me of all the responsibilities and go directly after Gaston who was now lawfully distanced from me.

By the time I was released from the hospital, I weighed less than a hundred pounds. And before I could stand on my feet, I had to regain my strength. During those difficult times, Elizabeth, Louise, and Hubert were at my side. While I moved in with Elizabeth, who nursed me back to health, Louise and Hubert gathered up my belongings from the village. So it was that I began a new chapter in my life.

CHAPTER 21

Starting Over

NOW THAT I HAD STEPPED OUT of seven years' worth of domestic abuse and farm life with Gaston, I was grateful that I had been given another chance. Since at this time I was in my mid-thirties, I reckoned to have reached the ripe old age of reason, meaning that I should start using my head instead of my heart. Naturally I needed to find a job as soon as could, for I left Gaston without a penny to my name. Then once I was settled, I promised myself, I was going to take writing classes and become an author.

Even if I wasn't sure which way I was headed, one thing was very clear, and that was that I was liberated from both Frank and Gaston. Although at the beginning Gaston was the catalyst for getting my children back, at the end he was equally responsible for chasing them out of my life. Under Gaston's domination all three of us had lost our self-esteem. Now it was time for each of us to make a conscious effort and rebuild our confidence. While

Harry had left home angry and hurt, Elizabeth was left feeling confused and betrayed. I don't think I gained any brownie points from my children for what I had put them through. I knew that I could never forgive myself for letting them down, and blamed myself a thousand times over for their continued suffering.

In spite my continued efforts to learn, my limited education and the lack of a diploma was a constant barrier to getting a decent job. But since I already possessed some hospital experience, I decided to continue my search in that direction.

As soon as I felt well again, I applied for a position at a large hospital in Montreal where, luckily, I was able to land a switchboard operator position. It didn't take me long to learn the corded switchboard system. Since I was good at my job, I was given excellent references when a short while later, I requested a transfer to the admitting office when a position came available. I was always aiming to better myself.

To my good fortune, the admitting supervisor was a British woman named Margaret who took an instant liking to me and hired me on the spot. I felt so fortunate to have connected with her, for she was elegant, refined, and cultured. I knew my mother would have completely approved of Margaret. Just being around her elevated my self-esteem. Her husband, who was a high-ranking officer in the British navy, was witty and entertaining. In some ways he reminded me of Winston Churchill. In short, the couple's vast cultural knowledge and their circle of interesting friends was an inspiration.

After Margaret's husband died, she was, for a time, on suicide watch. Since her two sons were both living abroad, I was literally the closest person to her, and as such, I was on constant lookout for her safety. This unfortunate incident caused us to become very close friends and we soon became an asset to each other. Margaret possessed a car, which gave us the opportunity to venture out on weekend trips and enjoy a wide range of recreational opportunities. We had many common interests: canoeing, skiing, theater, concerts, and movies. We took our miserable life in hand and made it better through joyous shared experiences. To me, Margaret was a godsend.

With my self-esteem and confidence restored, I gradually became more assertive at work and in my private life. I no longer allowed people to step all over me if I thought they were at fault. I was not afraid to defend myself. In fact, I think it's safe to say that I stopped being afraid—period. For the first time in my life, I felt that I had a right to be part of society. I felt liberated! Also, I was in my prime as a woman. Physically and intellectually I was at the peak of self-discovery.

Elizabeth and I rented a lovely flat in a nice neighborhood and when Harry came back he settled in with us. At last, the three of us were united without outside influence! I thought this would truly be the beginning of our happiness. But, alas, life is never that easy. All three of us had become damaged goods. Although our hearts were full of hope and love, we had sustained emotional trauma which was very difficult to overcome. It wasn't long before I realized that my wonderfully sensitive, loving son had returned like a wounded soldier, bitter and angry, bearing multiple scars, and justifiably blaming all his misery on me.

There was very little I could do to ease my son's heart since I was the cause of his bitterness. However, he did allow me to help find him a job, and with Margaret's connection at the hospital, he soon landed a position in the pharmacy where he was trained to assemble doctors' orders and deliver the drugs to the nurses' station. At last, Harry began to put the pieces of his life together, and even started dating. Now that we were all fairly settled at work and at home, I felt it was time to start thinking about taking a much-needed break. I was delighted when Elizabeth and her girl-friend Judy agreed to join me on a brief vacation in Jamaica. We were going to escape from the freezing Canadian winter!

CHAPTER 22

Jamaica and the Unforeseen Events

NOTHING ELEVATES ONE'S HEART more than the sight of palm trees and the sun after a long harsh winter. As soon as the three of us checked into a four-star hotel right on the beautiful sandy beach, we jumped into our bikinis and thereafter spent most of our days basking in the sun, drinking piña coladas and eating freshly cut pineapples sold to us right on the spot. In the evenings, we listened to calypso music, danced, and shopped in the local boutiques and felt as if we had been given a slice of paradise to taste and enjoy.

Feeling fit and beautifully tanned, we were sitting around in the lobby one evening when two young American men came over to us and engaged us in leisurely conversation.

Following the usual getting-acquainted chitchat, we learned that both men were drug enforcement agents working in Jamaica on a drug bust. Noticing how smitten Elizabeth was by one of them, when the men extended an invitation to drive us into town for dinner and dancing, I declined, not wanting to interfere or compete with my daughter. Since there was only sixteen years' difference between us, we were often mistaken for sisters.

Brad, the man who fancied my daughter, was in his early thirties. He was in the midst of a divorce, and was the father of three teenage children. Since in my eyes he was almost an exact clone of Gaston, I did not feel at ease in his presence right from the start. He was quick to inform us that though he was from the eastern part of United States, his current residence was in California, due to his profession.

When he first showed interest in Elizabeth, I was not terribly concerned, trusting that it would be geographically impossible for the relationship to come to fruition anyway. But as the weeks went by Brad's courtship became more intense, and his pursuit created a major conflict between Elizabeth and me. Like a peacock the man opened his colorful feathers to blind my daughter to his true identity, and it wasn't long before he completely captured her heart.

I sensed that this was not a good match for Elizabeth, but my protestations only alienated the two of us. Her suitor couldn't have been more pleased, since his aim was to have complete possession of her. A few months following their encounter in Jamaica, Elizabeth packed up and left for California, where she married Brad in a private ceremony without much ado. Knowing that I was opposed to their courtship, they neither notified me nor invited me to their wedding.

Meanwhile, Harry had also found his mate. He and his French-Canadian girlfriend organized a proper wedding. The celebration took place in a suburb of Montreal, and although I was invited to his wedding, there was an obvious detachment in my son's behavior.

This past year, which I had hoped would be a period of family bonding, had become instead a time of disappointments and increased estrangement.

It was ironic that for all the months I was Margaret's vigilante, protecting her from suicide, in the end it was she who gave me back my taste for life. With Margaret and Louise by my side for moral support, I was able to maintain my focus, my dignity, and the courage to move forward.

MY DEAR FRIEND MARGARET

Left without my children once again, I gave up my apartment and moved closer to the hospital where I worked. Margaret and I each had our own penthouse right next door to each other with a huge

215

MY DEAR FRIEND LOUISE

balcony and a magnificent view of both Montreal and the hospital. It was an ideal location! Not only did we have a glorious view of the city, but we could also see Mount Royal, the very mountain I fell in love with when I first arrived. For me, this was the best location in town, for it was in the center of everything I needed and wanted. I was but a half block away from work and only a few blocks from McGill University where I had since become a student of psychology and creative writing.

As I reflected on my past, it seemed as though my life had been more like a badly assembled quilt cover—random bits and pieces coming together in a variety of shapes and colors. And while I realized that there was nothing further that I could do for my children—for now they were both married and had begun building their own worlds—I remained determined to keep bettering myself so that when we all reconnected, they could be proud of their mother. They would see that I was strong, and that I was a survivor. I hoped that they would learn something from me.

Although I felt the worst was behind me, and I now had a relatively stable life, there was still one piece of the quilt missing: someone to love and for someone to love me. I needed to find someone meaningful in my life.

A couple of years after I started working at the admitting office, the hospital underwent some major leadership changes, at which time Margaret transferred to a sister hospital, while I got promoted to a secretarial position in a different department. Along with the changes came a new director, a young scholar with a Ph.D., who, as it turned out, was not only an expert in his field of practice, but was also a published author and a professor who lectured at the university. In addition to his medical expertise, he was also a fan of jazz.

As soon as Peter arrived in our department, he and I both felt a mutual connection. Everyone was pleased with his performance, and I, as the department's secretary, loved working under his direction. Right from the start, there was a subtle flirtatiousness that ignited between us. Although I am certain we were both fully aware of its ultimate ramification, neither of us made the slightest effort to quell our temptation. Since he entered into my life when I was lonely and most vulnerable, I carelessly ignored all the warning signs, not wanting to miss out on the opportunity to fall in love again.

I was in my mid-thirties, lonely and with a damaged heart. My children were both gone and had left with hard feelings. Elizabeth was devoured by her love for a possessive husband who made every effort to keep us at a distance; Harry had cut me out of his life, and was dealing with an addiction to drugs.

Although I did have my dear friends, Margaret and Louise, I still had a heart full of love yet no one to share it with. I wondered if my yearning to belong to another person might have had to do with the loss of my parents in my early childhood; and, after all, like everyone on earth, I too was made of flesh and blood and had unfulfilled feelings. This intense desire to be wanted and needed often left me confused between love and lust. In my general state of anxiety I was unable to differentiate between true love and just plain physical desire. I naively thought that when a man took me in his arms it was because he loved me, because I meant something to him—that it wasn't solely for his sexual pleasure.

Impressed by Peter's professional accomplishments and sharing his love of jazz, I quickly became an easy mark. Our romance began soon after his arrival. I knew next to nothing about his life outside of work, and he knew very little about mine. Since our relationship was based purely on a physical level, not an intellectual one, we were not much into conversation and never really asked many questions.

But I eventually woke up to the fact that not only was this man married, but he had been starting—or, at least, was trying to start—similar fires with other female employees within the hospital. In my anxiety to be loved, I had stupidly neglected to put up my guard. I was completely shocked to find that while I was desperately and madly in love with this person, he, on the other hand, saw our relationship as a casual fling, and me as a toy, to be tossed aside when a new toy became more attractive. In actual truth, I meant absolutely nothing to him outside of his sexual pleasures.

The realization of my downfall both infuriated and humiliated me. How could I have allowed myself to get entangled in such an unrequited romance, and with a married man, when all I was looking for was a monogamous relationship, some form of true allegiance with a person of the opposite sex. If not in my thirties, when was I going to learn? Surely there would have to be *one* single man out there worthy of my love? I was totally distraught and felt worthless, a perpetual failure.

Then one night, during my desperate hours when I generally went to bed crying, just as I turned out the lights I thought I heard someone come through my front door. In fact, I even felt a slight breeze! Frightened, I sat up almost afraid to look, but then I reminded myself that since my door was double-locked and chained I must have been imagining things. So I lay back down, thinking that perhaps from all the tears I was losing my mind when suddenly I felt a soft, gentle breeze blow right across my bed! This time it was not my imagination. I could definitely feel it! Feeling terribly frightened, I was about to pull the cover over my head, but I felt paralyzed—unable to move my hands. Then I felt someone sit by the side of my bed, someone who moved my pillow ever so slightly as if to make me more comfortable. Suddenly this presence felt very safe, as if it truly cared very much for *me*. Someone had come to comfort me.

Although at first I was terrified, it wasn't long before my fear dissipated along with the agony of sadness I had felt before. And as I lay still, I could gradually feel my heart and soul freed from personal anguish. I was left calm and content like a newborn, suffused in an eerie sort of otherworldly feeling. Then, as I lay under the spell of this peaceful bliss, I fell asleep. The next morning when I awoke, my depression had been lifted. My focus was clear and exact. All at once I knew what I had to do!

I realized that instead of looking for love from outside sources, I needed to love and accept myself for who I was. In other words, I needed to become my own parent. My mysterious nocturnal visitor somehow woke me up to the fact that we cannot rely on others to love us—that love and acceptance must come from within ourselves unconditionally.

The mysterious visit left me with the revelation that helped redirect my focus and brought a new perspective into my life. It became clear that I needed to move on and distance myself from that hopeless relationship. I resigned from my position at the hospital and found a job with an accounting firm nearby.

Although the distance to my new job was not much greater than it was when I worked at the hospital, since I was going the opposite direction, it was breaking my heart. Each day I had convinced myself that my heroic attempt at separating myself from my lover would pay off, and in the end I would be rewarded by knowing my heart and soul would be healthier. But not all wounds heal quickly, and I still found myself yearning for a call or at the very least a chance meeting on the street. Indeed, there were times when he would call and ask to meet me, and at those times I had to gather all my strength to resist the temptation to accept. How does one say no to heroin when one is addicted? That's how I felt about this person. Then I reminded myself of my mysterious visitor and gained strength from knowing that something or somebody out there really cared about me.

Since the firm I worked for had an office in Los Angeles, I begged for a transfer. Although they did not do that, they did give me a contact name that was very helpful. It was truly a stroke of incredible good fortune to be given a letter of recommendation for a job at a dental office in Beverly Hills, California. Had it not been for my daughter living in California, I would never have been able to summon the courage to make that long-awaited journey to America.

CHAPTER 23

America at Last

PACKING FOR MY MOVE TO AMERICA—the destination I had dreamed about for so long—was exactly the distraction I needed for my broken heart. My preparations didn't take long. Things I could not sell, I gave away. I did not want to keep anything that would have even remotely reminded me of the past. Not even a little stuffed animal my "friend" from the hospital once gave me. I was determined to wash the slate clean and this time around start a completely new life! In the end, I had no more than a single suitcase when I boarded the plane for Los Angeles.

My heart was filled with a profound sense of sadness. Not only was I leaving my son behind, but also my two best friends, Margaret and Louise, and, yes, of course, the man I hated to love. But I knew that it was the right thing for me to do.

*   *   *

America at last! I thought to myself, smiling, as I sat on the plane looking down at the miniscule houses below. Here I was, not only headed to the land of my dreams, but I was about to rekindle my relationship with my daughter. I was proud of myself for having gotten rid of all my possessions that would have only tied me down to painful memories. I felt incredibly liberated!

Before leaving Montreal, I had gone to say goodbye to Harry though we had not been in touch for quite some time. He was, as I had expected, seemingly indifferent about my decision to leave Canada. His lack of reaction reminded me of the way my relatives had been back in Hungary. Whether or not Harry cared, it was difficult to detect, since he showed no emotion. I sensed that even though it was he who rejected me, and oftentimes refused to let me visit his house, he felt abandoned once again and resented me all the more for my decision. I suppose in a way, subconsciously he liked playing the victim, for that somehow justified his long-held resentment—a resentment to which, I acknowledged, he was totally entitled. His wife made no effort to ease our strained relationship, making it more of a challenge for me to approach my poor son. It's not that I blamed Harry for his rejection—for I fully understood all the suffering he had to endure because of my mistakes, but what I could not comprehend was his failure to understand how much I needed him and his love. All I could do was pray that one day he would have a change of heart, and forgive me for my failures.

Even though both my children were grown up and married, my relationship with them had remained tense. Deep down, I knew, they carried a terrible feeling of abandonment. Neither Elizabeth nor Harry could let go of that feeling, or comprehend that they had been kidnapped and *not* abandoned by me as they were made to believe. As the years went by, they somehow learned to accept and live with this false concept; it became their comfort zone, so that their mistakes or difficulties in life could always be blamed on their terrible childhood. They seemed unable to move on. No matter how I tried to relate to them the actual facts of what happened, their minds were made up. To this day, I dare say, they choose to forgive me rather than accept the truth. Understandably, they have been dealing with a lot of anger, doubt, loss of self-esteem, and an abject sense of betrayal throughout their lives. Yet, in spite of all their scars, somehow we have managed to maintain a deep and abiding love for one another. We have finally come to live in peace. Despite the dark past that haunts us, we have learned to love each other unconditionally.

*   *   *

Elizabeth, who lived in the outskirts of Los Angeles, did her best to welcome me into her home in spite of Brad's lack of enthusiasm. Sensing his resentment, I quickly took measures to move out on my own and started looking for a place to live near my work. With the bit of savings I had accumulated, I purchased an old used car; I rented a furnished room in Beverly Hills. I was ready for my new life.

Although I had no experience in a dental office, Dr. Kovacs hired me based on the glowing recommendation I had received from my previous employer in Montreal. Not only was I offered the job as a dental assistant/secretary, but Dr. Kovacs helped me get my work papers, which was very providential. Before long I was settling in. I loved the warm winters, and the flowers all year round. I even made some new friends.

But all was not well, for regardless of my determined efforts, I still had to live with my broken heart. No matter the distance, I could not forget the man from whom I was running. It was an obsession. Since I had foolishly agreed to correspond, our letters only made me miss Peter all the more, and I found myself yearning for his mail as much I used to yearn for his physical presence. So when his invitation came for me to meet him in San Francisco, where he was attending a seminar, I recklessly jumped at the chance.

*   *   *

He was to meet me at the airport. I had carefully selected my outfit for maximum allure. My hair was styled to perfection, and my makeup was flawless. In short, the plan was to bowl him over with my good looks. But, true to his nature, upon seeing me, all Peter said was "You look spiffy." He never complimented me further, nor did he display the slightest bit of affection. Still, not wanting to let myself feel hurt, I chalked up his indifference to the time and distance that had come between us. Perhaps he was feeling guilty or uncomfortable in my presence? Or perhaps he really didn't care? It was difficult to know. We checked into the hotel where, surrounded by his colleagues, we were obliged to keep a reasonable distance and pretend that we were perfect strangers. All this time I stood nearby studying his face, wondering what attracted me to him. I could not come up with an answer. Questions started building up in my head. Why had I agreed to meet him? What were my expectations? I knew he was married, and I knew he did not love me—was I completely out of my mind? I could not understand my conduct. All the promises I made to myself seemed to have fallen by the wayside.

When at last we found ourselves alone in our room, I expected wild moments of passion, or perhaps a declaration of love—but all I got was an announcement that he would have sessions all day long and into the evening, and that he would not be able to spend much, if any, time with me alone during the day. Not even a single meal together. This time I truly felt like a cheap tramp! I could barely tolerate the humiliation. Naturally I tried changing my plane reservation to return home earlier but I was unsuccessful. My punishment for my stupidity was that I had to stay put and tolerate the pain and disgrace to which I had subjected myself. Once again I fell back into my mode of lack of self-esteem such as I felt with Gaston, where instead of taking an assertive action I subconsciously chose to become the victim and stayed, hoping that the next day would be different. That he would come to me, and we would make up and fall into each other's arms one last time.

After his seminar was over, we shared a taxi to the airport during which time not a word was exchanged between us. Then when it was time to head to our separate planes—me going back to Beverly Hills, he to Montreal—he said, "Well, I hope you have a good trip, and I hope I meet a sexy stewardess on the plane flying home."

His final remark went through me like a knife! It was exactly what I needed for my final awakening. It completely opened my eyes and closed my heart. I was forever cured.

Once back home, I reflected on what had happened and realized that my trip was not made altogether in vain for it taught me a very valuable lesson—I had to keep focused on my future and leave the past behind. I needed to maintain my self-respect and never, ever again allow myself to enter a meaningless relationship.

Months went by without news from my children. Elizabeth, who continued to be brainwashed by her possessive husband, kept her distance. It appeared that Harry, whose marriage fell apart, had forgotten about my existence. I didn't even know his address! Even the relationship between Elizabeth and Harry was strained.

Meanwhile, Dr. Kovacs was not entirely pleased with my performance, and since our feelings were mutual, I did not object when he asked me to resign my position. I was chagrined to realize that, contrary to what I had been made to believe, the pavements in America were *not* covered with gold!

Although my life was once again at a standstill, I was fully aware of the fact that the future was in my hands. It was up to me to make magic happen.

Fortunately, before long I was able to find work through a temp agency. After doing a series of office jobs, an opportunity came that led me back to my old profession, modeling. This was not an ordinary modeling job; it had to do with the opening of a new store on Rodeo Drive, the most prestigious of all streets in Beverly Hills. The store was called Juschi—so named, I suspect, as to be mistaken for Gucci.

By all standards, Juschi was the most exclusive, most elegant store anywhere in North America, surpassing even Gucci. It was even featured in the hit movie *American Gigolo* starring Richard Gere. With its red, genuine suede carpeting, brass stair railings, crystal chandeliers, and the elegant bar that offered free cocktails to its wealthy clientele throughout the day, it was truly a magnificent and innovative boutique for the elite of Beverly Hills. The European owners had come to California with the idea of catering only to the rich and famous—the movie stars and their high-powered agents and attorneys—and they were very selective when hiring their staff. One had to be above average in every way: attractive, elegant, educated, multilingual, and with excellent sales skills.

Opening night was equal to any Oscar event in this glamorous city. Guests were received on the red carpet with a glass of champagne served to them as they walked through the door. I was assigned as the "welcoming committee," positioned right up at the front door. All at once the movie stars were pouring in! Instead of my going to Hollywood, Hollywood was coming to me! It felt as if I stood at the gate of paradise. There I was, shoulder-to-shoulder with some of the stars I had admired and dreamed about for years. Vincent Minnelli, Richard Harris, Eva Gabor, Cyd Charisse, Tony Martin…all part of an endless stream of celebrities who had come to mingle and check out the store. As I stood handing out the champagne glasses, I thought, *Yes! I have arrived! This is America!*

I could hardly believe that I was part of such fame, elegance, and sophistication. Imagine—all these wealthy influential folks looking at *me,* admiring the mink coat and the pretty shoes I was modeling for them! Who would have thought this to be possible?

As I walked among these celebrity guests, politely smiling, modeling the exquisite high-end merchandise, I could not help but reflect back to my horrid past, and to think how remarkable it was that I had come full circle. I wondered what they would think of me if they knew that less then twenty-five years ago, I was wandering about the streets of Budapest, starved, with news-paper wrapped around my feet and a tattered turban covering my shaven head. Suddenly I felt like Cinderella. After all my trials and tribulations, I was none the worse for wear. I had come to a place in my life where I felt more confident and a lot wiser. At last I had become the person I was meant to be.

Was I walking in a dream? No, of course not. From the gutters of Budapest to the glitter of Hollywood—this was America! Just then someone asked me to show off the mink coat I had on. I turned to her with confidence. At that moment, I truly liked myself.

While I circulated amidst these fascinating people, modeling and showing off the finest furs, silks, and the latest styles in the prettiest shoes, I came to realize that these important folks were people, just like me. I had heard it said, and it seemed so cliché, but now I was finding it to be true—there was really no difference between the rich and poor. Famous or not, rich or poor, we all possessed the same qualities, the same flaws, the same fears; we breathed the same air. To me this was an astonishing discovery, one that instantly elevated my self-esteem. At the end of the day, no one is offered a shortcut to happiness; it's something that each person must achieve for himself.

The trouble with this extravagant project in the heart of Beverly Hills was that it was built on fraudulent financing. Soon after the elaborate opening affair, the creditors came knocking on the owners' door. Before long, it became known that the owners had a criminal record and had been jailed in Europe for fraud. Now, they were running their old playbook. Consequently, the store was quickly shut down. The party was over! The owners were deported, and most of the suppliers and employees were left behind unpaid.

Since my track record as a salesperson and as a model was of value in the fashion business, I quickly landed a job as a sales associate in a high-end ladies' dress shop located in Century City, adjacent to Beverly Hills. Later I became the store's manager.

But even though my life seemed relatively stabilized, I was still yearning for more, something stimulating, a creative outlet.

Although painting had long been my passion, I was ready to pursue my old desire to write, and signed up for a creative writing course at Beverly Hills High, one of their adult evening classes, It was a decision that forever changed my life.

CHAPTER 24

Finding my Soul Mate

LEN LIPTON, Ph.D., was already an accomplished writer when he came to join the Beverly Hills writing class. To this day, I cannot understand the reason for him being there, except that it had to be by some providence. Len had majored in film in college, he worked with Milos Forman on *One Flew Over the Cuckoo's Nest*, he taught film studies at the University of Southern California, and had a Ph.D. in communications. Yet in spite of all these impressive credentials, he showed up in my class as one of the students.

He sat across the table from me, and I could hardly take my eyes off him. There was something different about him, something both mysterious and appealing. I knew from the moment I saw him that he was unlike anyone I had ever met before. He was tall, dark, and quite handsome, with a wonderful deep voice. Although we made eye contact a couple of times during class, I firmly told myself to repress further thoughts of him, assuming that he was married, or, at the very least, had a girlfriend. But then when he approached me during the break and asked if I would join him for coffee after class, I fervently hoped that he was available.

In the restaurant we sat in a booth across from each other and casually chatted. And it became evident that he was indeed unattached and available. He was refreshingly different from Frank, Andre, Gaston, Peter. Len was genuine and he was honest. There were no dark ulterior motives. What a concept! I could tell almost from our first encounter that Len had a pure, kind heart. He was a man who was looking for a soul mate, and to my good fortune, he found me.

While we sat sipping our coffee and enjoying our apple pie, Len invited me to see a production of *Glengarry Glen Ross* costarring Jack Lemmon, one of my favorite actors, and since I loved the theater, and was happy at the prospect of spending more time with Len, I jumped at the chance. We had our first kiss in the parking lot that night, and from that moment on, our relationship just kept growing.

I think we both realized soon after we met that somehow we were destined to be together. As we went about sharing our daily existence—our walks in the park; watching the sun set; enjoying football games, movies, plays, museums, concerts, trips; our families and friends; our laughter and tears; our careers; and even our occasional fights—we knew that each of us brought something very valuable into the other's life. Len introduced me to his family, who even kept a framed picture of me on their mantelpiece! He stood by me and supported me while my children and I grew to forgive and love each other all the more. Len helped me study and guided me to become an American citizen.

AMERICAN AT LAST!

Then, one day—after thirty-two years of our life together—Len left me. He died of malignant melanoma. I cannot think why he was called away at such an early age—he was only sixty-four—except, perhaps, if reincarnated he was needed to save another lonely heart. For thirty-two years we were there for each other in sickness and in health. Len was my rock and my reason for waking every morning and for going to sleep at night. I could never have imagined my life without Len and I still can't. But sometimes destiny has its own agenda. I often thought of the moving words of Antoine de Saint Exupéry in *The Little Prince*:

> *"When he lights his street lamp, it is as if he brought*
> *one more star to life, or one flower. When he puts out*
> *his lamp, he sends the flower, or the star, to sleep. That*
> *is a beautiful occupation. And since it is beautiful, it*
> *is truly useful."*

I frequently wondered if Len had been sent to me as compensation for my horrid past. I guess I will never know. But what I do know is that this wonderful man gave me everything I was deprived of and needed all my life; he gave me true love and a sense of belonging. Ironically, had my heart not been abused and broken by my past mistakes, I would probably have never known how to fully appreciate his kindness.

CHAPTER 25

Present Time

As THE YEARS PASSED, my children each found happiness. Harry was divorced and then married a terrific woman who has become his true partner in life. In fact, it is thanks to his wife Suzanne's understanding and encouragement that Harry and I have reconciled and developed a true bond. Harry has learned to accept and like himself. His problems with drugs are long past. He has become a successful, well-respected business owner.

As I had expected, Elizabeth's marriage did not last. But out of that troubled marriage she was gifted with a wonderful child, a girl who has grown up and completed her studies at medical school; she is now a surgeon. Elizabeth herself is more accepting of her life and of herself. She still works for the airlines. I believe that she is now at a point where she has found some happiness in her own right.

Harry, Elizabeth, and I have become more understanding of what we all went through in our troubled lives. We have learned to love and accept one another, allowing our hardships to turn us into stronger and more compassionate human beings.

LEN & ME

As for Len and me, during our time together, we stood together for richer or poorer, through sickness and in health—a promise we made without any spoken words or the interference of any religious order. Len transformed me into a *somebody* by unconditionally accepting me for who I was. I knew that I was his woman. He was incomparable; he was one of a kind. I will miss him so long as I live. I will try and walk in his shoes—until we meet again.

*　*　*

Marika Roth

Marika Roth was born in Budapest, Hungary. After surviving the brutal Nazi occupation of her homeland, Marika immigrated first to Paris, then to Montreal, Canada, where she worked as a fashion model while studying creative writing and psychology at Sir George William University and at the Montreal School of Fine Arts. She continued on her path toward becoming a writer by taking courses at UCLA and at the Writers Boot Camp in Los Angeles. Marika is a member of Women in Film, a nonprofit organization whose purpose is to empower, promote, and mentor women in the entertainment and media industries. In addition to writing screenplays, Marika has had several art exhibits displaying her angel collections, both as paintings and as a collection of greeting cards, which were inspired by her beloved orange tabby cat Rasputin. Her acrylic-based figurative artwork has been shown at several private exhibits. She lives in Los Angeles.

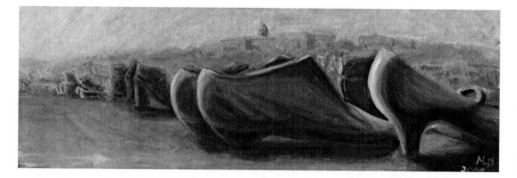

Title of painting: Budapest Holocaust Memorial II

ABOUT THE COVER ARTIST

Marcus Krackowizer

Marcus Krackowizer is a British artist currently living in the UK. He is a contemporary impressionist painter whose travels, especially to Budapest and Thailand, along with a long-term spinal injury, have greatly influenced his work. A self-taught original pallet knife technique results in richly textured, strikingly vibrant pieces. Be sure to check out more of his work at www.artoak.net where you can also purchase limited edition prints of the cover painting.

LaVergne, TN USA
09 February 2011
215910LV00006B/41/P